The Keeshond

THE
KEESHOND

BY ANNA KATHERINE NICHOLAS

© 1984 by T.F.H. Publications, Inc., Ltd.

ISBN 0-86622-032-1

Distributed in the UNITED STATES by T.F.H. Publications, Inc., 211 West Sylvania Avenue, Neptune City, NJ 07753; in CANADA by H & L Pet Supplies Inc., 27 Kingston Crescent, Kitchener, Ontario N2B 2T6; Rolf C. Hagen Ltd., 3225 Sartelon Street, Montreal 382 Quebec; in ENGLAND by T.F.H. Publications Limited, 4 Kier Park, Ascot, Berkshire SL5 7DS; in AUSTRALIA AND THE SOUTH PACIFIC by T.F.H. (Australia) Pty. Ltd., Box 149, Brookvale 2100 N.S.W., Australia; in NEW ZEALAND by Ross Haines & Son, Ltd., 18 Monmouth Street, Grey Lynn, Auckland 2 New Zealand; in SINGAPORE AND MALAYSIA by MPH Distributors Pte., 71-77 Stamford Road, Singapore 0617; in the PHILIPPINES by Bio-Research, 5 Lippay Street, San Lorenzo Village, Makati, Rizal; in SOUTH AFRICA by Multipet Pty. Ltd., 30 Turners Avenue, Durban 4001. Published by T.F.H. Publications Inc., Ltd., the British Crown Colony of Hong Kong.

Dedication

*To all Keeshond lovers and
their beautiful dogs.*

In Appreciation

To all of you who have contributed in any way toward the photographs and information contained in this book, we are deeply grateful.

Many of the older photographs are from my own collection. Others have been loaned for your enjoyment. We are proud of them, and feel them to be representative and interesting.

A special word of thanks goes to Hazel Arnold, my good friend from Houston, Texas, who has loaned me two recent editions of *A Breeders Guide to the Keeshond*, published by the Keeshond Club of America. These marvelous volumes have been of inestimable assistance in researching pedigree information, refreshing the memory, obtaining addresses, and in many other ways. Her generosity in providing me with this source, and allowing me to keep it for so long, is appreciated beyond words.

Carol Aubut has done a bang-up chapter on grooming and coat care, for which we extend gratitude. We feel that it will add much to the usefulness of this book to those exhibiting Kees.

Marcia Foy has put in endless hours helping with the correspondence, checking copy and proofreading, all of which is appreciated sincerely.

We hope that Kees lovers everywhere will enjoy this book, finding it interesting and informative.

Contents

About the Author

Since early childhood, Anna Katherine Nicholas has been involved with dogs. Her first pets were a Boston Terrier, an Airedale, and a German Shepherd Dog. Then, in 1925, came the first Pekingese, a gift from a family friend who raised them. Now her home is shared with a Miniature Poodle and a dozen or so Beagles, including her noted Best in Show and National Specialty winner, Champion Rockaplenty's Wild Oats, an internationally famous Beagle sire, who as a show dog was top Beagle in the nation in 1973. She also owns Champion Foyscroft True Blue Lou and, in co-ownership with Marcia Foy who lives with her, Champion Foyscroft Triple Mitey Migit.

Miss Nicholas is best known in the dog fancy as a writer and as a judge. Her first magazine articles were about Pekingese, published in *Dog News* magazine about 1930. This was followed by a widely acclaimed breed column, "Peeking at the Pekingese," which appeared continuously for at least two decades, originally in *Dogdom* and, when that magazine ceased to exist, in *Popular Dogs*.

During the 1940s she was Boxer columnist for the American Kennel Club *Gazette* and a featured East Coast representative for *Boxer Briefs*. More recently, many of her articles of general interest to the dog fancy have appeared in *Popular Dogs, Pure-Bred Dogs/American Kennel Gazette,* and *Show Dogs*. She is presently a featured columnist for *Dog World, Canine Chronicle,* and *Kennel Review* in the United States and *Dog Fancier* in Canada. Her *Dog World* column, "Here, There and Everywhere," was the Dog Writers Association of America selection for Best Series in a dog magazine which was awarded her for 1979. And for 1981 her feature article, "Faster Is Not Better," published in the *Canine Chronicle,* was one of four nominated for the Best Feature Article Award from the Dog Writers Association. She also has been a columnist for *World of the Working Dog*.

It was during the 1930s that Miss Nicholas' first book, *The Pekingese,* was published by the Judy Publishing Company. This book completely sold out two editions and is now an eagerly sought-after collector's item, as is her *The Skye Terrier Book,* published through the Skye Terrier Club of America during the early 1960s.

Miss Nicholas won the Dog Writers Association of America award in 1970 for the Best Technical Book of the Year with her *Nicholas Guide to Dog Judging*. Then in 1979 the revision of this book again won the Dog Writers Association of America Best Technical Book Award, the first time ever that a revision has been so honored by this association.

In the early 1970s Miss Nicholas co-authored with Joan Brearley five breed books for T.F.H. Publications. These were *This is the Bichon Frise, The Wonderful World of Beagles and Beagling, The Book of the Pekingese, This is the Skye Terrier,* and *The Book of the Boxer. The Wonderful World of Beagles and Beagling* won a Dog Writers Association of America Honorable Mention Award the year that it was published.

All of Miss Nicholas' recent releases from T.F.H. have been received with enthusiasm and acclaim; these include *Successful Dog Show Exhibiting, The Book of the Rottweiler, The Book of the Poodle, The Book of the Labrador Retriever, The Book of the English Springer Spaniel, The Book of the Golden Retriever, The Book of the German Shepherd Dog* and *The Book of the Shetland Sheepdog.* In the same series with the one you are now reading, Miss Nicholas has recently finished *The Maltese* and is currently working on several additional titles. In the T.F.H. "KW" series, she has done *Rottweilers, Weimaraners* and *Norwegian Elkhounds.* She has also supplied the American chapters for two English publications, imported by T.F.H. *The Staffordshire Bull Terrier* and *The Jack Russell Terrier.*

Miss Nicholas, in addition to her four Dog Writers Association of America awards, has on two occasions been honored with the *Kennel Review* "Winkie" as Dog Writer of the Year; and in both 1977 and 1982 she was recipient of the Gaines "Fido" award as Journalist of the Year in Dogs.

Her judging career began in 1934 at the First Company Governors' Foot Guard in Hartford, Connecticut, drawing the largest Pekingese entry ever assembled to date at this event. Presently she is approved to judge all Hounds, Terriers, Toys, and Non-Sporting Dogs; all Pointers, English and Gordon Setters, Vizslas, Weimaraners and Wire-haired Pointing Griffons in Sporting breeds and, in Working Group, Boxers and Doberman Pinschers. In 1970 she became the third woman in history to judge Best in Show at the prestigious Westminster Kennel Club Dog Show, where she has officiated on some sixteen other occasions through the years. In addition to her

Ch. Koenik Lewis winning the Non-Sporting Group under judge Anna Katherine Nicholas at Northwestern Connecticut Dog Club in 1959 for owner-handler Mrs. T. Whitney Peterson.

numerous Westminster assignments, Miss Nicholas has judged at such other outstandingly important events as Santa Barbara, Trenton, Chicago International, the Sportsmans in Canada, the Metropolitan in Canada, and Specialty Shows in several dozen breeds both in the United States and in Canada. She has judged in almost every one of the mainland United States and in four Canadian provinces, and her services are constantly sought in other countries.

Through the years, Miss Nicholas has held important offices in a great many all-breed and Specialty clubs. She still remains an honorary member of several of them.

11

DE GEWAPENDE KEES.

The Keeshond was a popular figure as the mascot of the People's Party back in Holland during the era of the French Revolution. Here is an example of a representation of a Keeshond made around that time.

12

Chapter 1

Origin and Development of the Keeshond in Holland

The Keeshond is a member of the Spitz family, a group of dogs whose mutual characteristics include upright ears, curled tail, a ruff or mane of hair framing the head and face, and only moderate rather than great angulation of the hindquarters. It is open to speculation as to when and how the dogs arrived in Holland, but it is generally agreed that they have been there "for several centuries," and assumed that their progenitors came on barges carrying coal and lumber from the Schwarzwald and Wurttemberg, or else crossed the border from Westphalia and the Rhineland to the Dutch provinces of Gelderland and Limburg. Specifically we have read that their direct forebears were the Wolf-Spitz and/or the Oversize Pomeranian. Strangely, our historical studies have taught us that the Keeshond is descended from the Oversize Pomeranian, while another authority states that the Pomeranian was produced by selective breeding of the Keeshond—which places emphasis on the close association of the early members of both breeds. Obviously they share a mutual background, the strain of dogs which has given us as well the Chow Chow, the Finnish Spitz, the Norwegian Elkhound, and the Samoyed.

Keeshonden have long enjoyed popularity in Holland, not only on the barges but as a family companion and a farmer's dog as well. Always a dog of the people, perhaps best known there as the "Dutch Barge Dog," "Foxdog," "Fik" (by the southern provincials), and "Kees" in the northern provinces. The name Keeshond is probably most frequently mispronounced of any in the canine world. Correctly it is spoken "Kays-hond" and means quite simply Kees-dog. The breed is said to have been named for Cornelius De Witt or for

13

Cornelius de Gyselaer, noted patriots of the 17th and 18th centuries respectively, or possibly in honor of both. "Kees" is short for "Cornelius," and the Keeshond became the mascot (or Keezen) of the People's Party, so what more likely than that they may have been named for one of these men? Those who protest the truth of this say that the name "Kees" is synonymous with "Spitz" which refers to "rabble," and since the Kees are of Spitz descent, does this not also seem logical?

The political problems brought to Holland by the French Revolution had their effect on dogs as well as people. Especially the Keeshonden dogs, who owing to their identification with the Patriots (even to the leader, de Gyselaer, owning one) fell promptly from general favor with the defeat of their party. It was almost as though their owners were embarrassed at being seen with a mascot of the "wrong" political faction. Sadly, many owners quietly rid themselves of their Kees dogs, particularly in the crowded cities. The Pug Dog, symbol of the House of Orange which had been victorious, continued to prosper.

Fortunately for the future of Keeshonden, the country people's outlook was more of loyalty to their dogs; the countryside still was well supplied with them, many lovely ones being seen on the farms and in homes. Thus it was that when the Baroness van Hardencroek became an admirer of the breed and wanted to raise some of these lovely dogs, she was able to find handsome ones available in the possession of the farmers. These provided the foundation for her very famous Walhalla Kennels established with the breeding of her first litter.

Miss J.G. van der Blom of Holland was another early Dutch breeder.

The Dutch Keeshond Club was formed in 1933, and due largely to the efforts of Baroness van Hardencroek, De Raad Van Beheer op Kynologisch Gebied in Nederland accepted the standard for the judging of the breed that same year.

Early Kees came in various colors. The gray variety is said to have originated in the southern provinces, Limburg and Brabant. There were blacks, too, back in those days, which later became extinct in Holland; and whites over a goodly period of time were extremely popular, especially in Gelderland where often it seemed as though they were outnumbering the grays. This variety was no longer admitted as a Dutch Keeshond when the Dutch Standard of Points was revised.

Following is a translation, from the mid-1930s, of the Germano-Dutch Standard of Points for the Keeshonden:

GENERAL APPEARANCE:—A short, compact alert looking dog with a fox-like head, small pricked ears, and a well curled very bushy tail showing a good plume. A full coat and loose but very dense ruff. The hair on head, ears, muzzle and legs is short and sleek.

HEAD: Well proportioned to the body. Seen from above, the skull is wide, gradually tapering towards the nose in the form of a wedge; sideways, the head should show a definite stop. The muzzle should not be unduly long or too snipy, nor too blunt, coarse or heavy. The nose must be black, small and round. A so-called "ram's" nose is an asset. Lips should not overlap. The lips and the rims of the eyes should be black, even in white Keeshonden. The ears should be small, neatly placed, close together, triangular in shape and pricked, carried erect and set on high. Eyes should not be too big or prominent, but almond shaped and obliquely set. They should always be dark.

NECK AND BODY: Neck should be fairly long. The back as short as possible and very straight. Extremely cobby in appearance. Well-sprung ribs and barrel well rounded.

TAIL: Of fair length, set on rather high, rising straight up and bending over the back to curve either to the left, or to the right, in a circle lying close to the body; or curled tightly on the back.

LEGS: Of medium length, sturdy and very straight. Hocks only slightly bent.

FEET: Small, round and cat-like.

COAT: Short and smooth on head, ears, feet and inside fore-and hindlegs; thick and long on other parts of the body. On neck and shoulders the hair should be loose and outstanding, forming a ruff or mane. The coat should never be curly, wavy or woolly, nor should it form a part down the back. Most abundant around neck and on tail. The forelegs should be feathered from elbow to knee. On the hindlegs the feathering should stop just above the hock, the legs being short-coated below.

COLOUR: The Grey Keeshond should be either wolf-grey, silver-grey, ash-grey, or tawny and should have a light undercoat with long, black tipped, outstanding hairs. The muzzle should be dark, and there should be dark markings described as "spectacles" around the eyes. The belly and tail should be of lighter colour.

These are white (a color recognized in the Netherlands as allowable for Keeshonden) Keeshond puppies named Aurora Bianca and Adonis Bianco, sired by Int. Ch. Kavancha's Now or Never and bred by Mrs. Pam Fedder of Welkom, South Africa.

IN BLACK KEESHONDEN: The undercoat and often the skin are dark. The outercoat should be a glossy blue-black without white or any other coloured patches.

THE WHITE KEESHONDEN: Should be pure white, without any yellow markings.

SIZE: Grey Keeshonden, both for dogs and bitches, should measure 18 inches at the shoulder, the larger the better, but size should not prejudice type.

Black and White Keeshonden should measure 16 inches at the shoulder.

FAULTS: A blunt nose, or so-called "swine" nose. A flat skull (like an Alsatian's) giving a wolfish appearance. "Appleheadedness," meaning an unduly rounded skull. Long, large or drop ears, placed wide apart. Tail carried too loosely, or too gaily, high above the back, or drooping, in fact not lying close to the body. Curly, woolly, wavy or silky coats, or coats showing a parting on the back. Dew-claws on hind legs. Flesh coloured noses, eyelids or lips. Light or large protruding eyes. An excessively dark face or a completely black muzzle. Black patches on forelegs (so called "thumb marks"), and black or white patches on body or legs.

The first Dutch Specialty Club and the German Specialty Club recognized what they described as "other colours," which included all additional colors except parti-color, the latter being white dogs with distinct black or brown patches. Colored dogs with white socks or white markings on chest were allowed.

An interesting note is that at one time, during the past century, it was not uncommon to see Keeshonden in Holland shaved in the manner of a Poodle. Numerous political prints of that period depict the Kees dogs in this manner.

Returning to the subject of the early standard: by the 1930s it had been decided that the "Dutch" Keeshond must measure *under* 18 inches at the shoulder where formerly the gray variety was to be *"at least* 18 inches" shoulder height.

Recently we have run across an article written by G. De Josselin De Jong, of Haarlem, Holland, stating that (in about 1962) the F.C.I. (Federation Internationale Cynologique, governing body of several dozen countries where canine affairs are concerned) ordained that the Keeshond's Country of Origin be transferred from Holland to Germany, on the grounds that the Dutch Kees, having become nearly extinct at one period, it had become necessary to import German blood in order to perpetuate the breed, while at the same time German breeders were bringing dogs from Holland to blend into their breeding programs. Obviously the writer of that article was disapproving of the whole thing and of the explanation that so much interbreeding had caused the dogs to become ONE type—the German type. In the past, it is explained, there had been two definite strains, the Dutch and the German. The German dogs, it was said, had larger ears and were coarser than the Dutch, and these dogs were known as "the Pomerania Kees" and the "Dutch Kees" respectively. This same article goes on to state that the dwarf of the former, known as the Spitz of Pomern, kept the name of "Pomeranian."

This article was written in 1965, and I would imagine that the F.C.I. action would have caused considerable furor among the Dutch people. Somehow or other I feel quite certain that no matter who ordains what, in the minds of the public the Keeshond will always remain the Dutch Barge Dog, and the National Dog of Holland!

17

The original of this Gainsborough hangs in the Wallace Collection, London. Called *Perdita*, the painting is of a white Keeshond; white was a popular Keeshond color at that time.

Chapter 2

The Keeshond in Great Britain

In Great Britain, the Keeshond Club was organized in 1925, several years earlier than a similar event that took place in Holland. And while the Baroness van Hardencroek was assembling what turned out to be foundation stock for a noted kennel in Holland, Miss Hamilton Fletcher, who was to become Mrs. Wingfield Digby, was making a yachting trip in the Dutch canals, saw and loved the handsome barge dogs, and brought back a pair. She did not realize that they were a distinct breed at the time of purchase; but when the first litter arrived, somewhere in the early 1900s, she noticed that type of the puppies was far too consistent for them to have been mongrels.

Mrs. Wingfield Digby is generally credited with being the person who introduced Keeshonden in Great Britain. Actually, however, as long ago as 1816 there have been printed references to the "Fox Dog," "Wolf Spitz" and Pomeranian. It is believed that the dogs who as early as pre-1916 were exhibited as "Overweight Pomeranians" were in reality the progenitors of later generations of Keeshonden, and the period following the Kennel Club's cancellation of all Challenge Certificates for "Overweights," in 1916 until the 1920s, found little or no mention of these dogs. "Overweights" of that period ranged between 16 to 30 pounds.

Following the close of World War I, the breed was first registered in England under the name of "Dutch Barge Dog." In October 1925, with Mrs. Wingfield Digby receiving both the offices of President and Secretary, the Dutch Barge Dog Club was founded. The following year the name was changed to The Keeshond Club. Mrs. Digby continued over many years as a breeder of quality and the importer of

A group of the van Zaandam winners of the early 1930's with Miss Wingfield Digby, daughter of the owner.

judiciously selected stock with which to enhance the quality of her dogs. The first two "Dutch Barge Dogs" to be shown in England were Breda and Saani, both owned by Mrs. Wingfield Digby, at the National Dog Show in Birmingham. In 1925 she purchased Hendrick van Zaandam from Germany; and in 1928 Cornelius van Zandaam from Holland. The many "stars" in her kennel included Champion Konstant van Zaandam, born in 1931, a multiple Certificate winner; Champion Bartel van Zaandam, bred by Mr. Schmidt, born in 1923, who became the property of Mrs. J.C. Moore and won a first Certificate in 1928, completing title in 1930; Champion Lutine van Zaandam, a homebred owned by Colonel and Mrs. Wingfield Digby, born in 1933, a daughter of Champion Gosina van Zaandam, became a champion the year following her birth; and Champion Kendrik van Zaandam, an especially gorgeous dog who took Best in Show at the 1934 Keeshond Club Specialty among other prestigious wins, a homebred in which to take pride! Kendrik was by Hendrik of Worton from Kenau van Zaandam (by Alli von der Sternwarte ex Champion Gosina van Zaandam who finished in 1931 and was the dam of Champion Dochfour Hendrik and other champions).

The Baroness Burton, becoming interested in Kees during the mid-1920s, acquired Champion Dochfour Hendrik, a very famous and beautiful dog who is said to have attracted great favorable attention to the breed. He was the first Keeshond to complete a British championship. Another purchase, during the 1920s by the Baroness, was Dochfour Egbertina, who had started life in 1926 bred by the Wingfield Digbys, as Egbertina van Zaandam and was by the German importation Hendrik van Zaandam ex Traes van Zaandam.

Eng. Ch. Lutine van Zaandam, a homebred belonging to Mrs. Wingfield Digby, owner of the famed van Zaandam Kennels, the lady who introduced the breed in Great Britain. Lutine gained title at an early age in 1934.

Mrs. W.A. (Alice) Gatacre was very active in the Keeshond world and a well respected fancier. She imported, bred, and exported a goodly number of handsome dogs, and her "Guelder" Kees are in the background of at least several important early American kennels. Additionally Mrs. Gatacre is author of an early book on the breed. Among her important winners was Champion Ado v Thierlstein, bred by Mrs. T. Lehman, born in 1927, who gained his first Challenge Certificate in 1929 and by 1933 was the holder of four Challenges plus numerous additional honors.

Mrs. J.C. Moore brought an important dog from Germany, Black Bock, who became the sire of champions and eventually belonged to Miss Hastings. Mrs. Moore also owned Champion Bartel van Zaandam and imported Bertie von der Maiblume among others.

Miss Hastings became very famous, deservedly, through her "Evenlodes," a number of whom were successful imports in the United States and Canada, providing foundation stock to breeders.

Mrs. Norton was a hard working Honorary Secretary of Britain's Keeshond Club in the mid-1930s, and was owner of the gorgeous bitch Champion Viva Ten Eyck, who gained what might be called a whirlwind championship in 1932-33.

It would be impossible to find, in all our dog show world, a kennel more completely respected, nor one which has contributed more to the progress of a breed, than the famed Wistonia Keeshonden owned by Nan and Fred Greenwood. Although Wistonia is now located at Lawndale, California, basically it is an English Kennel, for England is where it began, and where so many of this breed's most magnificent members were bred. One has but to glance through the kennel stories of this book to note the beneficial impact the Greenwoods and their dogs have had on the Keeshond as we know the breed today. Dog after dog, generation following generation, QUALITY was found there and this quality is being carried on today at many a kennel whose breeding programs are based on Wistonia.

Special commendation is due Nan Greenwood not only for the marvelous type Kees raised in her kennel but also for her kindness to newer breeders, her willingness to help them get off on the right foot, and the encouragement she has always given, and still gives today. A very outstanding dog lady, just as Wistonia is a very outstanding line of superb Keeshonden!

Mrs. E. Scroggs of the Ledwells is a current English breeder with some exciting accomplishments to her credit. Her most famous dog without a doubt is the fabulous English Champion Ledwell Dutchman, a once-in-a-lifetime dog, who died in 1983 leaving a fabulous heritage by which to be remembered.

One in a litter of eleven puppies by Champion Han's Silver Mist ex Ledwell Catastrophe (she a litter sister to the dominant and important American and Canadian Champion Racassius of Rhinevale and to English Champion Ledwell Charlotte), Dutchman was sold as a show-prospect puppy at age eight weeks to Mrs. D. Purdo, for whom he did some nice winning in the puppy classes as he matured. Then at thirteen months he gained his first Challenge Certificate, completed title at eighteen months, and by the time of his retirement had won 26 Challenge Certificates under 26 judges, thus beating the previous record holder for most Challenge Certificates won by a Kees, Champion Volkrijk of Vorden. The latter had been the only Kees to attain the honor of Supreme Champion at Crufts.

Like all truly GREAT dogs, Dutchman left his mark as a stud as well as in the show ring. A daughter of his litter sister, Champion Ledwell Charlotte, was bred back to him, producing a son who nearly equalled Dutchman's record in the show ring. This is Champion Ledwell Lysander, owned by Mrs. Jean Sharp, who retired Lysander on winning his 25th Challenge Certificate, not wanting his record to exceed that of his sire. Both dogs were bred by Mrs. Scroggs. Champion Ledwell Lustre of Keesland, noted producing bitch, was also from the combination that produced Lysander.

A Rhinevale bitch and Dutchman produced Champion Rhinevale Roustabout and Champion Rhinevale Rachmaninov, while Champion Waakzaam Wurzel and Dutchman became parents of the important winner Champion Waakzaam Wursling.

To many Dutchman's most memorable win was that of first in the Utility Group at Crufts in 1976.

Mrs. Margo Emerson owns the Rhinevale dogs, who are known and well admired in the United States and Canada.

Mrs. Anne MacDonald is another noted British breeder with superior dogs to her credit. Her Hanovarian Kennels are located at Faversham in Kent, where three of her current champions we have the pleasure of picturing for you.

Champion Hanovarian Zeus of Ven, six years old as we write, was an outstanding puppy winning consistently, gaining more than thirty firsts at Championship Shows between the ages of six months and a year. He is the only Keeshond, his owner tells us, to have won three

Eng. Ch. Zorba of Von Hanovarian is a son of Hanovarian Twilight and bears a strong resemblance to him. Owned by Mrs. Anne MacDonald, Faversham, Kent, England.

Eng. Ch. Hanovarian Zeus of Ven holds the record of 98 Junior Warrant points; he took eight Challenge Certificates as a yearling and holds numerous C.C. awards. Mrs. Anne MacDonald of Faversham, Kent, England owns this dog.

Eng., Am., and Can. Ch. Wrocky of Wistonia here is taking Best in Show at Santa Barbara Kennel Club in 1955 under the late Col. E.E. Ferguson, handled by Porter Washington for Flakkee Kennels, Lawndale, California.

Championship Show Puppy Stakes outright, on one occasion defeating more than 400 puppies. Also he was the only Keeshond to qualify for the Pup of the Year Competition, unfortunately losing coat just then and winding up third. He holds the record of 98 Junior Warrant points, took eight Challenge Certificates as a yearling, and presently holds nine Challenge Certificates and ten Reserve Challenge Certificates. He was more or less withdrawn from the ring in favor of his younger brother, Zorba, and his son, Champion Hanovarian John Boy who were in the wings awaiting their opportunity. Zorba and Zeus were sired by the late Hanovarian Twilight who was also the sire of Champion Duroya Honesty and Australian Champion Duroya Homeguard.

Over the years, Mrs. MacDonald has made every effort to concentrate on soundness, good necks, definition of color, masculine males and feminine bitches. As she says, "It doesn't always turn out exactly as I would like, but if one doesn't try to produce type and soundness it will never be achieved."

Champion Hanovarian Spring Mist was the only homebred bitch Mrs. MacDonald has had which became a champion, but, she comments, "I must admit that I get much more fun out of showing dogs." When a dog has completed title, Mrs. MacDonald doesn't find it nearly so interesting to continue showing that dog, but much prefers starting again with something new.

Mrs. MacDonald further comments "I don't like exporting unless I know the people to whom the dogs are going. I only export to Ray and Marilyn Porter in Australia (see Australian chapter) because we think on the same lines, and I will only send them something if 100% sure it is what they need at the time."

Mrs. MacDonald breeds only once or twice each year, since hers is strictly a hobby kennel. She is a popular judge, both in the United Kingdom and overseas, who thoroughly enjoys the dogs she gets to see on these assignments.

Although she keeps her dogs strictly as house pets, Mrs. MacDonald is proud of the fact that in 1976 and 1978 hers was the Top Kees Kennel in the U.K., and that she owned the Top Brood bitch in 1968 and the Top Dog in 1978.

It was in 1968 that Mrs. MacDonald acquired her first Keeshond, and her first Kees champion. Hanovarian Spring Mist was from her first homebred litter born in 1969, a previous Kees litter, in 1969, having been on "breeder's terms." Prior to the Kees, Mrs. MacDonald owned German Shepherd Dogs, and now Lowchens, not yet recognized in the United States, share her interest as a breeder with the Kees.

England's Top Keeshond breeders for 1982 were Gina and Bob Weedon, whose Keesland Kennels at Brixham in Devon have achieved considerable fame although being a small operation. Mrs. Weedon's belief is that the Keeshond is responsive to living in the small family unit, and so they usually have approximately four females (at present all males are sold). It is for this reason that several of the Weedon champions are owned by other keen exhibitors, in order that each dog be placed so as to enjoy family companionship.

Only one or two litters are bred annually at Keesland, and only top winning bitches are used for this purpose. In but ten years' time, the Weedons have bred seven English champions, with several others overseas. Very nice going!

Gina Weedon feels that the strength of the kennel has been due to the bitch line, the foundation of which was Champion Ledwell Lustre

English Ch. Hanovarian John Boy, a son of Ch. Hanovarian Zeus of Ven, one of the current winners belonging to Mrs. Anne MacDonald, Faversham, Kent, England.

of Keesland, bred by Mrs. R. Scroggs. Lustre was a line-bred daughter of Champion Ledwell Dutchman and Champion Ledwell Heidi. Mated to her half brother, Champion Rhinevale Rachmaninov, she produced Champion Keesland Ember, who won the bitch C.C. at Crufts in 1978, and also Esmerelda, who won three Reserve Certificates, and Endeavour, who won a Challenge Certificate offered by the Federation Cynologique Internationale towards a dog's championship in Holland.

For her next breeding, Lustre was mated to another leading stud dog, Champion Gelderland Clipper of Swashway. From this came the outstanding Keesland "F" litter, which included four champions out of the seven males and two females born. Champion Keesland Fenella of Bodarin, now owned by Mr. and Mrs. Quinn, was Top Challenge Certificate-winning Kees bitch in the United Kingdom for 1981 and 1982. Champion Keesland Firefly, English and American Champion

Eng. and Am. Ch. Keesland Fisherman at eight weeks old, whelped in 1979, by Ch. Gelderland Clipper of Swashway ex Ch. Ledwell Lustre of Keesland. Owned by Mrs. C. Downs, England.

Keesland Fisherman, and Champion Keesland Flipper of Lekkerbeck also made history, and the four together comprise the only four English Champion Kees bred in one litter to have earned for their dam the Dorcas of Evenlode Brood Bitch Cup for three years; 1980, 1981 and 1982.

Champion Keesland Ember, Lustre's daughter, won the bitch Challenge Certificate at Crufts in 1978; then, when bred to Champion Gelderland Clipper of Swashway produced the lovely Champion Keesland Gypsy, who in turn was mated to Sam the Candyman. This gave the Weedons their current "star," Champion Keesland Highlight, Top Challenge Certificate winning bitch in 1983, having a total to date, at eighteen months, of seven Challenge Certificates and one Reserve Certificate, having started out by gaining her very first at seven months of age on her debut at a Championship event. Highlight is a litter sister to Canadian Champion Keesland Hi Jacker, owned by Brenda Brookes. Lustre, Ember Gypsy and Highlight comprise a four-generation line of winning bitches.

The most recent Crufts' Dog Show as this is written was held in February 1983, judged by the all-'rounder Mr. Douglas Appleton who drew an entry of 66 dogs including nine champion dogs and seven champion bitches. Best of Breed, and the dog Challenge Certificate were awarded to Champion Gavimir Nighthawk, bred and owned by Mrs. Luckhurst, who truly had a super day as this dog went on to win the Utility Group; his son, Gavimir Kiang, was reserve dog Challenge Certificate winner, and a puppy owned by her, Traza Teasel, was reserve bitch Challenge Certificate winner.

In bitches, the Challenge Certificate was won by Duroya Irresistible of Dargrant owned by Mrs. Homes and bred by Mrs. Woodiwiss.

English Ch. Ledwell Dutchman snapped at a show in England in 1975. Dutchman is the winner of 25 Challenge Certificates and the sire of English Ch. Ledwell Lysander who has also won 25 Challenge Certificates but was retired from further competition by their owners who did not wish Dutchman's record to be surpassed, even by his own son! Both dogs were bred by Mrs. Sylvia Scroggs, Lysander's owner. Dutchman belongs to Mr. and Mrs. William Purdon. Photo courtesy of Tess and Bill Eckhart.

Shown here at ten years of age is Nancy Riley's famed and beautiful bitch Ch. Wallbridge's Best Bet, who made a major contribution to the breed as a producer back in the 1960s.

Chapter 3

The Keeshond in the United States

Keeshonden have been in the United States for a comparatively short time as one considers other breeds of dog. It was a young man from Stuttgart, Germany, Carl Hinderer, who in 1923, at 23 years of age, decided to join his sister in the United States, in Baltimore, Maryland. As soon as possible after his arrival here, and becoming settled, he sent home for his Kees—two dogs and two bitches—who arrived during Autumn 1926. It was then he learned that the breed was not yet recognized by the American Kennel Club, a fact which might have discouraged many. Not Mr. Hinderer, however. He bred several litters from his "Wolfspitz," each time registering the puppies with his club in Germany and obtaining German pedigrees for them, in compliance with the American Kennel Club rules.

In 1928 Mr. Hinderer joined the Maryland Kennel Club, and started attending smaller shows in that area.

On his way for a visit home to Germany, accompanied by his wife and a favorite dog, Wachter, Mr. Hinderer decided to stop off at the American Kennel Club to become personally acquainted with Dr. John De Mund who was President there at that time. Dr. De Mund obviously was impressed favorably with both the young man and his dog, for Mr. Hinderer left with instructions to bring back the necessary information and papers from Germany to start the groundwork for A.K.C. recognition of these dogs. Upon his return to the States, and at Dr. De Mund's request, Mr. Hinderer translated the Standard into English and agreed to the name "Keeshond" by which the breed was known in Holland. And so it was that in 1930 Keeshonden were officially recognized by the American Kennel Club, classified as "regardless of color" and relegated to the Non-Sporting Group. The first of the "new breed" were entered at the Maryland Kennel Club Dog Show on January 31st and February 1st 1930, six of them.

The first Keeshond registered with the American Kennel Club was the German bitch (the first six importations to the States came from Germany), Bellan von Trennfeld, daughter of Champion Geron am Ziel ex Hilde am Ziel, bred by Herr Franz Schwab of Trennfeld, owned by Mr. Hinderer.

To our knowledge, the last dog show that Mr. Hinderer attended was in November 1934. We understand that his dogs were hard hit by the epidemics so common in the dog show world of that period (prior to present day vaccines), with heartbreaking losses for him. Wachter, his beloved companion who had so impressed Dr. De Mund, lived to be fourteen years old, then was poisoned. It saddens us to learn of a gentleman who did so much to further the best interests of a breed having received so much misfortune through the dogs! I understand that after Wachter was gone, he never owned another Kees.

The breed received some very favorable early publicity at the beginning of the 1930s, which, together with the handsome appearance of the dogs and their attractive personalities, led to considerable interest in them. A rush to import some from England followed, and competitively the breed was on its way!

One of the first big American kennels was that of Mr. Irving Florsheim in the Chicago area, which became famous as home of the Red Top Kees. Mr. Florsheim's first selections came from among England's most prestigious breeders, bringing over for foundation stock such dogs as Dochfour Jasper from the Baroness Burton, this a son of Champion Ado von Thierlstein, bred by Mrs. W.L. McCandish. Four came soon thereafter from Mrs. Alice Gatacre's kennel: Guelder Chinchilla, Guelder Petrucia, Guelder Primrose and Guelder Silver Witch. Then two from Mrs. Wingfield Digby: Taal van Zaandam and Gerard of Evenlode, the latter of Miss Hastings' breeding. Dochfour Jasper and Chinchilla did some nice winning at Westminster in 1932 for Mr. Florsheim, as did Geraad of Evenlode and Guelder Petrucia, the latter taking Winners Bitch, at Westminster 1936.

Mr. and Mrs. Richard Fort, at Pleasantville, New York, maintained a very busy and successful kennel, with Harry Hartnett handler for their conformation dogs. They owned Champion Herzog of Evenlode,

C.D., who was the first obedience trained Keeshond in America, an imported dog bred by Miss Hastings by Champion Bingo ex Dorcas of Evenlode, born August 19th 1934. Also Champion Prestbury Sister, by Champion Dochfour Jacob ex Catherine de Witt, bred by Hon. Lady Cooper; Champion Black Peter, a homebred by Birtsmoreton Jon from Black Orania, born 1931, Champion Annie von Sander (a daughter of the noted English Champion Halunke of Evenlode, (litter brother to Herzog) and numerous others.

Mrs. Herbert C. House, of Farmington, Connecticut, was an important early fancier too, who based her kennel on fine imported stock. She owned Guelder Child of the Mist, Guelder Grey Dawn, Guelder Pearly King, and Guelder Seamist, all from the famous kennels of Mrs. Alice Gatacre.

An early 1930s exhibitor was Mrs. Kenneth Fitzpatrick, from California, who was showing Corri Van Fitz, a homebred at Westminster in 1937. This dog was by Dynasty of Canford ex Guelder Fitzpatrick, and he was born in September 1935. The Fitzpatricks had some sensational Kees winners over the years. It was from them that the lady who became Mrs. Porter Washington purchased her first one.

Those popular and highly respected Philadelphians, Dr. and Mrs. Henry Jarrett, who were Chow enthusiasts as well, became very active in the Kees world during the early 1930s. They owned the fine importation Gerolf of Evenlode, purchased from Mrs. Hastings. And it was the Jarretts and the Florsheims who organized foundation of the Keeshond Club, of which Mrs. Jarrett became an early Secretary.

During the 1940s interest in Kees was progressing at a growing rate. Mrs. J. Whitney Peterson had started her Nederlan Kennels at Greenwich, Connecticut, and was on the way to becoming an outstanding authority, breeder, judge, and author on the subject of Kees. A dedicated and knowledgeable person, her contributions to the breed were inestimable. Among the dogs who made her kennel famous were Champion Nether-Lair's Banner de Gyselaer, Champion Nederlan Keesa van Banner, Champion Nederlan Winston of Wistonia (bred by the Greenwoods), Champion Nederlan Panda v Kirk, and many, many more.

During the 1940s, too, Champion Wynstraat's Kerk brought Keeshonden into the limelight by becoming a Group winner here in the East. Bred and owned by Mrs. Jean O. Vincent, Wynstraat Kennels, Millbrook, New York, Kerk was handled to nearly all of his important victories by Albert J. Meshirer. Sired by Champion Hans

Ch. Wynstraat Kerk, owned by Jean Vincent and handled by A.J. Meshirer, was the East's first consistent Group-winning Kees back in the late 1940's.

Brinker Van Sander ex Champion Tassel of Artel, Kerk was born on September 14th 1947. Wynstraat Kennels bred an impressive number of champions in addition to Kerk, who was a very admirable sire, his progeny including Champion Nether-Lair's Banner de Gyselaer, Champion Dirdon's Durk Donder, Champion Lousanne's Folly's Pride, Champion Dirdon's Flitsen Komeet, Dutch Holiday of Paumanake, C.D. among others.

Kerk's sire, Champion Hans Brinker Van Sander, was by the Forts' Champion Herzog of Evenlode C.D. ex Fatima van Sander. He was born in 1942, bred by Mr. and Mrs. Jere R. Collins, then of Long Island, who eventually moved to England and I believe continued breeding and owned Kees over there. Mr. Collins was a "second generation dog fancier," his parents, Dr. and Mrs. Collins, having been famous breeders of some splendid Smooth Fox Terriers.

34

Tassel of Artel, Kerk's dam, was born December 1945, by Champion Cim van Sander ex Champion Bobsno's Sister Dinky. She was bred by Martin W. Feigley who showed a number of Kees here in the East during that period and earlier. Both of Kerk's parents had been purchased by Mrs. Vincent who exhibited them during the late 1940s. Champion Sim van Sander, Kerks' maternal grandsire, was owned by the Collins, by Champion Herzog of Evenlode C.D. ex Champion Prestbury Sister, and was bred by Mr. and Mrs. Fort.

Annie R. Adams was a consistent exhibitor of Keeshonden during the early 1940s often having three or four of them at the shows. One of her dogs, originally called Dirk, who was born in 1941 by Duk Weddil ex Gay Tamezak, was eventually sold to Mrs. Russell S. Thompson for whom he became Champion Dirk Adams and sired Champion Wynstraat's Cover Boy, U.D.

Mrs. Thompson was closely involved with the Keeshond world in those days as secretary of The Keeshond Club. Another handsome dog belonging to her was Champion Dirdon's Durk Donder.

Virginia Ruttkay's dogs were already winning in the 1950s (as with Flakkee and some of the other long-lived earlier kennels, you will find a kennel story on these later on).

Ned and Betty Dunn Cummings were early Kees breeders and professional handlers who had a very worthy succession of Kees in the rings over the years. Their dedication and splendid presentation of their dogs was widely admired, as was their work in obedience.

Marye E. Picone had Champion Dirdon's Helder Zwier, C.D. and Champion Dirdon's Wonder Wander Hocage, both of them sons of Champion Wynstraat's Kerk, out as "specials." Mrs. Peterson was competing with Bacchus of Evenlode, an import, some good young bitches, and her several noted "specials." Mrs. Fitzpatrick had Champion Van Fitz Bingo, and Flakkee had Wrocky of Wistonia on the West Coast. Van Ons Kennels were showing. So was Mrs. Philip Rosen.

Albert Meshirer, who handled Kerk to his exciting record, was a Kees breeder himself as well (and a breeder of Boxers).

Mrs. Nancy P. Riley is a long and dedicated Kees breeder and enthusiast, starting in the 1950s. It was in 1961 that she acquired future champion Wallbridge Best Bet, ROMX, as a stud fee puppy from the breeder, Betty Lou Wallbridge. Best Bet became the Top winning Kees Bitch of 1965, during which year she was shown 21 times as a "special" and won Best of Breed eight times (with Group placements

Ch. Windrift's Lover Boy, one of the many outstanding Kees from Joanne Reed's famed Windrift Kennels, Canyon Country, California. Now owned by Les Baker, New York.

on four of those occasions) and Best of Opposite Sex some half dozen times. Best Bet was the breed's Top Producing Bitch from 1966 until 1983. Bred a total of three times to three different stud dogs, she produced eleven champions, and provided the foundation stock for a number of important kennels. Her progeny includes famous Best in Show and Group winners. She was the dam of the very famous Champion Von Storm's Emerson Prince Piet among others, who was sired by Champion Nederlan Herman v Mack.

Champion Von Storm's Emarice, Best Bet's daughter by Herman, was bred and owned by Nancy Riley. She was the Top Winning Kees bitch of 1966, and held a position in the Top Three from 1963 through 1965. Her exciting victories in the show ring included Best of Opposite Sex at the National in 1965, the Capitol Kees Club Specialty in 1965 and 1967, the Devon Specialty in 1966, and she was undefeated in her sex during 1966. As a "special" shown seventeen times, she was consistently either Best of Breed or Best of Opposite Sex, and had several or more Group placements to her credit. She was also the dam of champions.

Champion Wallbridge's Best Bet was by Champion Nether-Lair's Bard de Gyselaer ex Champion Kenmerk's Heiress.

Ch. Von Storm's Emerson Prince Piet, Best in Show winner, was in Top Ten All Breeds one year during his career. By Ch. Nederlan Herman V. Mack ex Ch. Wallbridge's Best Bet. Pictured at a Keeshond Club of America Specialty judged by Mrs. Evelyn Silvernail, handled by Roy Holloway. Bred by Mrs. Nancy P. Riley, owned by Mr. and Mrs. E.P. Hempstead.

Mr. and Mrs. E.P. Hempstead of Greenwich, Connecticut, were very much in the thick of keenest competition with their important and handsome dogs Champion Nederlan Herman v Mack, who was born in 1959, by Champion Baron Mack of Keeshof ex Champion Vursa of Winston, bred by Mrs. Peterson, and Herman's son, Champion Von Storm's Emerson Prince Piet, who was also Best Bet's son and bred by Nancy Riley. These two dogs, together and individually, swept the boards at important Eastern shows, winning together as a very outstanding brace, and separately as "specials" very much in evidence in the breed, Group and Best in Show categories. Roy Holloway handled these two, who surely reigned supreme for quite a period of time.

Ch. Nederlan Herman v Mack, owned by Mr. and Mrs. Emerson Hempstead and handled by Roy Holloway, winning Best in Show at the Wilmington Kennel Club in May 1965.

Ch. Baron Mack of Keeshof winning the Non-Sporting Group at National Capital Kennel Club in 1962.

(Left to right) Nancy P. Riley with Ch. Von Storm's Emarice on the left. Mrs. J. Whitney Peterson, judge. Roy Holloway with Champion Herman v Mack.

Ch. Japar Fearless Knight, handled by Joy S. Brewster, takes a good win from Miss Gwladys Groskin at Camden County Kennel Club around 1970. Dr. and Mrs. Benjamin Ackerman, owners, Hollywood, Florida.

Mr. and Mrs. John A. LaFore, Jr., were outstanding Kees enthusiasts prior to Jack LaFore becoming President of the American Kennel Club, at which time they discontinued exhibiting. This was not too long after acquiring a dog I enormously admired, Champion Waakzaam Wollenhoven, born in 1966, a son of Waakzaam Wotan ex Waakzaam Wonderlick, bred by Mrs. E.M. Smyth. While he was campaigned by the LaFores, Roy Holloway handled this stunning dog, and continued to do so after he was sold to Mr. and Mrs. Stuart Duncan.

Another Kees memorable to me as I mentally review the past was Champion Japar Fearless Knight, owned by Dr. Benjamin and Mrs. Edna Ackerman, at that time from Connecticut who later moved to Florida, then retired from exhibiting as Mrs. Ackerman had become busy and popular as a judge, the role in which she is now best known to the Fancy. Fearless Knight came from the Japar Kennels in Ohio, the type and quality of whose dogs I have long admired, and was a son

Ch. Wallbridge's Best Bet, ROMX, bred by Betty Lou Wallbridge and owned by Nancy P. Riley, who acquired her as a stud fee puppy. A Top Winning Bitch of 1965, bred to three different studs, she produced eleven champions; her progeny formed the foundation for at least several leading kennels.

of Jane Parshall's Champion Dalbaro Beachcomber (Champion Vondel Handyman ex Waakzaam Sieglinde) from Champion Japar Candytuft. Handled by Joy Brewster, "Gus" made a deservedly splendid record in keenest East coast competition during the early 1960s. The Ackermans, who had formerly been important breeders of Silky Terriers, had another handsome Japar dog also winning for them, but "Gus" was the star of their Kees family and a bright one!

Mar-I-Ben Kennels, also from Ohio, had some splendid dogs I have admired, too. The frequency with which Champion Mar-I-Ben Licorice Twist turns up in important pedigrees speaks for itself!

The Richard Hollamans were loyal and successful Kees breeders who could be depended upon for quality. Charles F. Visich was well represented as an exhibitor by Champion Flakkee Sky Wrocket and Champion Von Storm Kimberly among others.

In Texas, Hazel Arnold, who is "into" numerous breeds including Kees (Poms and Beagles and American Foxhounds among the others), has shown me gorgeous Kees quality through the years. And from California, Robin Stark's success with her Star-Kees dogs (and her talents and ability as a writer) has gone down in Kees history and will continue to do so.

Eloise Geiger has provided foundation stock to many a new breeder. Jane Doty, whose mother, Margaret Gray, has owned and bred some of the nation's finest and most successful Skye Terriers, also has been a Keeshond owner and exhibitor over a period of time.

There are literally hundreds of dedicated people who have been involved with the Keeshond and its progress here in the States. I recall Doris McKee with some handsome dogs at Eastern shows. Pat Marcman, too. Bill Gamer (from upstate New York) with Champion Shady Hills Frederick and other dogs. We wish that it were possible for us to write of each of them and every dog in detail!

Feeling, as we do, that there is no better way to describe the progress of a breed of dog than by bringing our readers the stories of individual breeders who have contributed along the way, and of those who are currently active, we have selected a cross section of them with which to supplement our chapter on breed history in the United States. We present some of them who have current leading winners and summarize the background from which they have been produced. These kennel stories have become one of the most popular features of my T.F.H. books, and we are certain that in the Kees, too, there will be no exception!

Ch. Mar-I-Ben Licorice Twist winning Best in Show at Canton, Ohio, in January 1964. Eloise W. Geiger and Marilyn Bender, owners. Mrs. Geiger handling. Maxwell Riddle judging.

Ch. Wallbridge's Best Bet at twelve years of age. Owned by Nancy P. Riley, Millport, New York.

Chapter 4

Some Well-Known Kennels of Kees in the United States

A kennel name is important to a breeder, and should be elected and used from the time of one's first homebred litter. Kennel names are chosen in many different ways. Some people select for them the name of the street on which they live. Others will use a form of their own name, or a coined combination of the names of members of the family. Some will name the kennel for a child, or children, who may be especially enthusiastic over the dogs. Many use the names of the foundation dogs behind a breeding program, either the proper names or call names of these dogs. Whatever strikes your fancy, is appropriate and not burdensome, and infringes on no other person's rights is fine, and will identify you and your Keeshonden—especially important in those you yourself have bred, through future generations.

A kennel name can be registered with the American Kennel Club, which gives the registrant the exclusive right to that name in registering dogs, and no other breeder or owner may include it in the registered name of one of their dogs without written permission of the registrant during the period in which the registration of it is effective. You can receive detailed information regarding this procedure by contacting the American Kennel Club, 51 Madison Avenue, New York, N.Y. 10010. There are specific requirements regarding the type of name eligible for registration, and a fee is to be paid if one chooses this course.

To be of greatest value, kennel names should be applied to all dogs bred by your kennel, as then it immediately identifies the dog and its background. A good way is to work out a system by which your homebreds will bear names BEGINNING with the name of your kennel while dogs purchased from others and already bearing ONE name will have that of your kennel added at the END—or whatever other system appeals to you as a way to indicate whether the dog was actually BRED BY YOU, or was purchased.

Fairville

Fairville Kennels, owned by Mrs. Marguerite Goebel of Chadds Ford, Pennsylvania, was established back in 1958 when Mr. Goebel promised their two children, heartbroken over the loss of the family pet, a Cocker Spaniel, that each each could have a puppy of his or her own choice. Dog books and magazines were read and studied; kennels were visited; but it was actually at the Devon Dog Show that the Goebels' son, Richard, decided that he would like to have a Keeshond.

Virginia Ruttkay was there with her dogs, and the Goebels discussed the breed with her, making a date to come and see some puppies the following day. The Goebels' daughter came along, too, and when the day had ended, a five-month-old male had been purchased for Peggy and a two-month-old female for Richard. Mrs. Goebel was obligated to campaign the male to his championship, breed the two of them, and return two pick puppies to Mrs. Ruttkay.

Little did Marguerite Goebel realize, at this point, that she had embarked on a life-long hobby, and that her life style as a result would change completely!

"Soot" (Ruttkay Nigrescence) became a champion at the Lancaster Kennel Club Dog Show in 1961, where Mrs. Goebel met Jane West, and told her that she (Mrs. Goebel) was looking for a good female. Mrs. West was expecting a litter from English and American Champion Wilco of Wistonia ex her Champion Ruttkay Winsome (half Wistonia) and Mrs. Goebel was indeed fortunate to get Rhapsody of Westcrest from this litter.

In the meantime, Mrs. Goebel had fulfilled her obligation to Virginia Ruttkay, who had first and third pick puppies out of the seven produced by the dog and bitch the Goebels had purchased from her. One from this litter became Fairville's first homebred champion, although not reflected in the name, Champion Ruttkay Sabot of Clareton owned by Mary O'Connor.

Rhapsody was an instant success in the show ring, going from puppy class (at ten months) to Best of Opposite Sex to Best of Breed at the

Ch. Rhapsody of Westcrest, ROM, taking Group 1 at Mason and Dixon Kennel Club under judge Mrs. Leonard Bonney, April 1962. A consistent winner and the dam of six champions born May 18 1961, by Eng. and Am. Ch. Wilco of Wistonia ex Ch. Ruttkay Winsome, bred by Jane V. West and owned by Mrs. Marguerite K. Goebel, Chadds Ford, Pa.

Capital Keeshond Club Specialty in 1962 over six highly ranked bitch "specials," including her dam, under breeder-judge Marge Cummings. Three weeks later, owner-handled, Rhapsody came from the class to Group 1 under Mrs. Bonney at the Mason-Dixon Kennel Club Show. She finished with her fourth "major" at Wilmington.

Shortly before the foregoing, Fred Greenwood of Wistonia Kennels had come here from England. He advised Mrs. Goebel to write to his

Ch. Gallant Guard of Fairville, by Ch. Colonel Cinders of Fairville ex Birthday Babe of Fairville, placed in Group en route to title, shown here taking Best of Winners at Harrisburg Kennel Club under judge Mrs. Paul Silvernail. Steve Shaw handled for breeder-owner Mrs. Marguerite K. Goebel, Chadds Ford, Pennsylvania.

Ch. Bryn Haven Ingen of Fairville, by Am. and Can. Ch. Nederlan Herman v Mack ex Ch. Rhapsody of Westcrest, winning at Land O'Lakes, June 1969, under judge Howard Tyler. Marguerite Goebel, owner, Chadds Fork, Pennsylvania.

Lucky Leo of Fairville, Best of Opposite Sex in Keeshond Club of America Futurity 1969. By Ch. Colonel Cinders of Fairville ex Ch. Fantasy of Fairville, became a champion and a Group placing dog. Bred by Marguerite Goebel, later sold to Ruth Nichols.

wife in England about breeding Rhapsody, noting that she was the "pedigree expert." Nan Greenwood replied that Rhapsody should be mated to a son of Wilco, and since English, American, and Canadian Champion Wrocky of Wistonia was his best son, arrangements were made and Rhapsody took the trip to Flakkee Kennels in California where Wrocky lived and was owned by the Porter Washingtons. Three male puppies resulted, one becoming Champion Colonel Cinders of Fairville (sire of eight champions); another, Champion Commander Coal of Fairville; and the other went to owners who showed only occasionally.

Rhapsody, mated to English, American, and Canadian Champion Whiplash of Wistonia produced three females and two males. Fantasy and Fantom were Best in Futurity and Best of Opposite Sex at the 1966 Keeshond Club of America Specialty. Fantasy finished at Bucks County Kennel Club with four "majors." Fantom finished at Bryn Mawr that year. Frivolity, sold to a new home, also quickly gained the title.

In Rhapsody's litter of three by American and Canadian Champion Nederlan Herman v Mack were Intermezzo of Fairville, Best of Opposite Sex in the 1967 Keeshond Club of America Futurity, judge Jane West; and a dog who also gained the title.

Cinders and Fantasy produced the Fairville "L" litter. Lucky Leo was Best of Opposite Sex in the Keeshond Club of America Futurity in 1969, and then went to Miss Ruth Nichols who had just lost her Champion Gallant Guard of Fairville, a Group placing dog. Leo finished quickly, and Lively Lad also became a champion. Lorelei was more than halfway through to championship when she was injured and had to be put to sleep. Fortunately, Mrs. Goebel still had Lovely Lady, whom she bred to Champion Wistonia Wivenhoe. This produced Champion Nimble Nina of Fairville and Novel Nola of Fairville. Nola, bred to Champion Lively Lad of Fairville, produced two puppies, one of whom became Champion Odin of Fairville, Winners Dog at the National Specialty in 1976.

Nimble Nina, bred to Champion Maverick Son of Ilka, produced five puppies. One is American and Canadian Champion Pied Piper of Fairville owned by Jean and Tom Toombs, and beautifully presented by Jean. Another is Mrs. Goebel's Champion Prize Package of Fairville, and two more in the litter are pointed.

Fairville has, from the beginning, been strictly a "hobby" kennel, and it has been Mrs. Goebel's custom to breed a litter only when she

Ch. Colonel Cinders of Fairville shown finishing title at Salisbury, Md., November 1964. Owned by Marguerite Goebel, Chadds Ford, Pennsylvania.

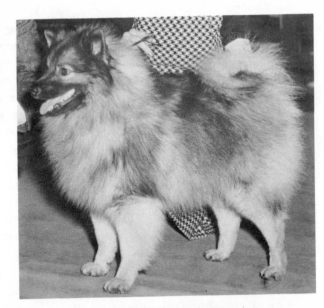

Ch. Lively Lad of Fairville taking Best of Winners for four points at Penn Treaty Kennel Club in 1971. Lively Lad, by Ch. Colonel Cinders of Fairville ex Ch. Fantasy of Fairville, finished at Harford County Kennel Club in 1973. Marguerite K. Goebel, owner, Chadds Ford, Pennsylvania.

needs to have something new coming along for the shows. Mrs. Goebel's dogs have the first O.F.A. (Orthopedic Foundation for Animals) numbers in the breed; she had taken them all to Dr. Riser to be X-rayed at the University of Pennsylvania as soon as the program was started there. Actually Mrs. Goebel had been X-raying since 1961, but was somewhat disconcerted when she took these X-rays to the University of Pennsylvania at the beginning of their program only to find out that the dogs previously had been improperly positioned. And so a return visit was made for Dr. Riser to do the dogs in the correct manner, and the O.F.A. numbers were assigned.

Rhapsody having been three-quarters Wistonia background, Mrs. Goebel chose to breed along that line. She was very successful, as fourteen champions and a C.D. title have been earned thus far by Kees bred at Fairville Kennels.

Ch. Nimble Nina of Fairville, by Ch. Wistonia Wivenhoe ex Lovely Lady of Fairville, owned by Marguerite K. Goebel, Chadds Ford, Pennsylvania.

Flakkee

Flakkee Kennels are synonymous with the finest in Keeshond type and quality, not only in the United States but wherever throughout the world the breed is known and discussed. The name as a kennel prefix came into being when Mrs. Van Cott Niven, (now Mrs. Porter Washington) decided to start showing dogs, the breed she admired and wished to own was the Kees.

Through Mr. Stearns, a dog broker, Mrs. Niven sought the services of a professional handler—one who could and would give her dogs first call in the show ring. Mr. Stearns contacted Porter Washington. An appointment was arranged, and Porter for the first time saw a Keeshond, a dog by the name of Patriot Van Fitz, that Mrs. Niven had purchased from Mrs. Vera Fitzpatrick, a noted Kees breeder of that period.

Naturally, never before having seen one, Porter had little knowledge of the breed when he and this Kees started out together. Kees were practically unknown in the California rings then. But one look at Patriot told Porter that this was a SHOW DOG—sound and beautifully coated, although a bit too light in color according to our present modern standards. Porter was making plans to go on the Arizona-Rocky Mountain Circuit, so he told Mrs. Niven that he would like to take Patriot along to try him out, allowing the judges an opportunity to indicate whether or not the showing of this dog would prove worthwhile.

Since there had been no competition in the breed, making it to the Non-Sporting Group was a simple matter. Patriot placed in the first two Groups and in the third, at El Paso, Mr. Earl Adair placed him first. From then on, until the end of the circuit, Patriot placed in every Group. By now Porter was thoroughly convinced that he had a potential winner, and so he entered Patriot in the coming Los Angeles Kennel Club Dog Show, which was held in the old Gilmore Stadium. Porter has never forgotten that day, as it became a milestone for the breed in North America when Patriot won the Best Keeshond, then the Non-Sporting Group under Richard Kerns, and then the supreme honor, Best in Show under Dr. Joseph Redden.

It was now time for a registered kennel name. Several Mrs. Niven had chosen had been rejected by the American Kennel Club for one reason or another. Finally it was decided to take a map of Holland and search it for names appropriate to a Keeshond kennel. One which she and Mr. Washington thought sounded well was "Flakkee," the name of a little island just off the coast of Holland. So application was made for this, and granted—the start of a most prestigious family of winning Keeshonden located in California.

Having now a Best in Show dog, Mrs. Niven felt that her next step should be concentrated on finding a suitable bitch to breed to Patriot. Looking through the English *Dog World* Annual, she noticed with admiration a picture of a young English bitch, Champion Whimsy of Wistonia, owned and bred by Mr. and Mrs. Fred Greenwood of the famed Wistonia Kennels. Several letters and a few phone calls later, Whimsy became the "new English import at Flakkee," and was eventually bred to Patriot, as had been Mrs. Niven's original intention.

Whimsy, to Porter Washington's knowledge, is still the only Kees in history who NEVER was defeated in the breed. She had won two Bests in Show in England before her departure for America; then at her very first show here carried right along by winning Best in Show that day from the open class under the late Anton Korbel, at the San Antonio Kennel Club. From there she added still another Best in Show, at Abilene, Texas. Shown in the States a total of fifteen times, her impressive record was five Non-Sporting Groups and two Bests in Show.

Another bitch, English Champion Wrona of Wistonia, was imported from the Greenwoods, this one also taking a Best in Show her first time in the ring here. Her show career was a short one, however, as she had been purchased specifically for breeding to a young son of Whimsy and Patriot, Champion Flakkee Dusky Devil. Some very nice progeny came from the combination, but still Mrs. Niven and Mr. Washington were not quite satisfied and were seeking better.

When the Greenwoods sent word that they had a gorgeous dog, English Champion Wilco of Wistonia, who had won the Stud Dog Trophy for three straight years in England, whom they felt should join the Flakkee stud force, this was arranged and Wilco was brought here. Looking him over upon his arrival, Mrs. Niven and Mr. Washington felt that this was the type dog they wanted and intended to produce, and from that point a strict line-breeding program was set up and has been adhered to right until the present moment.

Prior to the start of Wilco's American show career, Porter Washington spent many hours training him to perform in the show ring in the manner required for important winning. It took a bit of doing, as the dog obviously had been permitted to set his own rules. Porter's patience proved well worthwhile, and by the time Wilco's training period was completed, Porter could set him up, toss the lead over his back, and relax—knowing that the dog would continue to hold the pose until Porter indicated he should move. In what had become the family tradition, Wilco also took Best in Show the first time ever shown in America, and went on to win other Best in Show awards and several Groups before being placed in semi-retirement as top stud dog in Flakkee Kennels.

Of Wilco, Porter Washington has written: "This great dog without doubt has put the stamp on all good Kees in this country for type, size, color, temperament and soundness."

Prior to his departure for America, Wilco sired one of the breed's most outstanding members, Wrocky of Wistonia, who as a very young dog had gone to his English championship undefeated. Visiting the Greenwoods, Mrs. Niven had seen Wrocky at their kennel in England, and returned home with this dog foremost in her mind. Telling Porter about this glorious Kees, she said that she truly believed the dog to be the best of the breed she ever had seen. After much discussion, it was decided to make an offer on him, hardly daring to hope that the Greenwoods would actually be willing to let him leave their kennel. But they did, to the delight of his new owners.

By the time of Wrocky's arrival here, Mrs. Niven had become Mrs. Porter Washington. Thus Wrocky became their honeymoon dog.

Wrocky, too, was Best in Show on his debut here, and became an American Champion that same week by winning two more Non-Sporting Groups, going on soon thereafter to Canadian championship as well. Appearing in the North American show ring on only 36 occasions, Wrocky's brilliant career brought him a total of 35 times Best of Breed, 33 Groups in Canada and the United States, and a total of eighteen Bests in Show, these including such important and prestigious events as Santa Barbara and Pasadena among others.

Wrocky was shown only eleven months in the United States and Canada. His show career rather abruptly ended when he developed a cancerous testicle which necessitated removal of the faulty gland. This, however, did not impair his ability to sire puppies, and Champion Cornelius Wrocky Selznick was proof of this fact!

"Corny," as this Wrocky son was known, was also a multiple Best in Show and Group winner. But his most famous, and valued, accomplishment was his siring of the Top Winning Best in Show Keeshond in the History of the Breed, the noted Champion Flakkee Sweepstakes.

Ch. Flakkee Jackpot, the winner of 32 Bests in Show, 85 Groups, and 147 times Best of Breed. Owned by Mr. and Mrs. Porter Washington, Flakkee Kennels, Lawndale, California.

Opposite page: *(Above)* The great Ch. Flakkee Sweepstakes, whose record stands at 46 times Best in Show, 109 Group Firsts, and 165 times Best of Breed. Mr. and Mrs. Porter Washington, owners, Lawndale, California. *(Below)* Ch. Cornelius Wrocky Selznick, eight times Best in Show, 42 times Best Non-Sporting Dog, 87 times Best of Breed. Owned by Mr. and Mrs. Porter Washington, Flakkee Kennels, Lawndale, California.

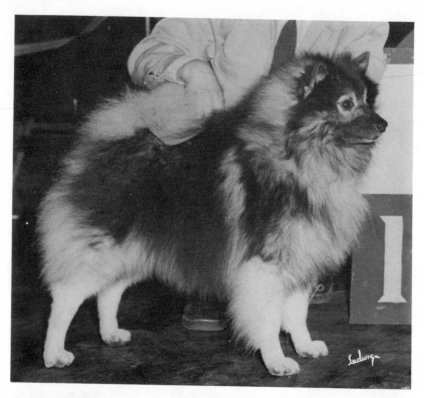

Eng. and Am. Ch. Wilco of Wistonia, winner of two Bests in Show, is another splendid Kees to have figured in the development of Flakkee Kennels.

"Sweeper" won a total of 46 Bests in Show, 109 Groups, and was Best of Breed on 165 occasions. Campaigned fearlessly in stiffest competition from coast to coast, Sweeper twice gained the Quaker Oats Award (in 1967 and again in 1968); was honored by *Kennel Review* magazine as Top Western Show Dog for 1967; and is still the ONLY Kees ever to have won the Non-Sporting Group at Westminster.

The next "star" to be presented by the Washingtons was a young male whom they named Flakkee Jackpot, who was sired by another importation from the Greenwoods, Champion Worrall of Wistonia. This dog, Worrall, had been sold to a man in Scotland as a pet, but it came to the Washingtons' attention that an American handler visiting Scotland from the States was trying to buy the dog for a client here. Mr. Greenwood was contacted by phone, and arranged to call on the man in Scotland and see the dog immediately. He liked what he saw, and since Worrall was closely related to the Flakkee breeding stock, felt that the Washingtons should have him. Arrangements were made and the dog sent over. Worrall arrived in excellent condition, and as Joan Ludwig, an extremely talented dog photographer, was at the Washingtons' when Porter returned with him from the airport, he

Ch. Worral of Wistonia, a three-time Best in Show winner, imported and owned by Mr. and Mrs. Porter Washington, Flakkee Kennels, Lawndale, California.

trimmed him up and Joan made a picture of him which turned out so well that it is the one always used in his standing pose.

Worrall finished in short order after having won the Non-Sporting Group at his first American show under Mrs. Ramona Van Court at the Antelope Valley Kennel Club. It is unfortunate that this splendid dog was never given the chance his quality deserved: that of becoming a great winner in American show rings. But this was the period during which the Washingtons were vigorously campaigning their famous Pomeranian "Sparky," who thus always took first call over Worrall when both won their Groups and were eligible for Best in Show competition, Porter always handling the Pom himself. However, Worrall more than made up for this in other ways. The one uppermost in historic value is the fact that it was he who sired the dog the Washingtons feel had the strongest impact of any of his breed in this country until his time: the immortal Champion Flakkee Jackpot. "Sonny," as Jackpot was known to his host of friends, came into being as the result of Caroline Merchant visiting Flakee one day. She brought with her a bitch of the Washingtons' breeding seeking their advice as to the correct stud dog for her. One look convinced Porter that this had to be the perfect mate for Worrall, who had not as yet been used since his arrival in America. To quote Porter, "This very nice lady took my advice, and the mating was made."

After the breeding, Porter suggested that Mrs. Merchant bring the puppies to the kennel following their birth and he would remove the dewclaws and make suggestions on the rearing of the litter. In due time Mrs. Merchant called and announced that her bitch had whelped a lovely litter; on their third day she brought them for the dewclaw removal. Porter was truly impressed with the puppies when he saw them, and asked Mrs. Merchant to bring them for him to see at eight weeks.

When the day came, he was literally on "pins and needles" awaiting their arrival. Nor was he disappointed! After carefully examining each of them as they played and moved about in an exercise pen he had placed in the driveway for this purpose, two were selected to join the Flakkee kennel. They were named Flakkee Jackpot and Flakkee Baccarat, and became known as Sonny and Cher.

What followed was canine history! Jackpot became the third Top Winning Kees in History, and although Baccarat hated dog shows, she became a famous dam through producing Flakkee Replica who is the dam of three Best in Show Kees—the only member of her breed thus distinguished. These are Champion Flakkee Hijack, America's Top Winning Kees for 1979, and Champion Silver Frost Huggy Bear owned by Mrs. Patricia Armstrong, these two sired by Replica's uncle, Champion Flakkee Jackpot. And Champion Flakkee Snapshot, Top Kees in 1981, sired by Champion Flakkee Instamatic.

Today Jackpot appears in almost every pedigree of the outstanding dogs in the country. His most famous son is the Top Group Winning Kees in History, Champion Flakkee Instant Replay, known as "Speedy," who has been Best of Breed on a total of 221 occasions; won 146 Non-Sporting Groups, and been Best in Show 45 times. Porter and Dickie Washington comment: "He could no doubt have broken Sweeper's record; but there was a lot of sentimentality involved regarding Sweeper, so we preferred to just let the records stand as they are."

Instant Replay likewise did his part as a sire, producing the famous Champion Flakkee Instamatic, who was the Top Winning Kees in America during every year he was shown, namely 1977, 1978, and 1980. He was shown at Westminster and placed second in a very fast Non-Sporting Group under the late Peter Knoop.

Instamatic, in his turn, sired the current "star," Champion Flakkee Snapshot, America's Top Winning Kees for 1981 and a heavy contender for the top spot in '82. His offspring are now standing in the wings, awaiting their turn to show the Kees world that they, too, can do it in the Flakkee manner!

As of February 1st 1983, Flakkee-bred and Flakkee-shown Keeshonden have won a total of 1192 Bests of Breed; 586 Non-Sporting Groups; and 185 Best in Show awards. The Washingtons believe this to be a record unsurpassed! Looking toward the future, hopes are high for the career of Flakkee Snappy Tom by Snapshot from a Champion Flakkee Knockout daughter.

In retrospect, another fine dog that was imported to Flakkee from Wistonia Kennels was English and American Champion Waarborg of Wistonia. This dog had eight Best in Show wins and many Non-Sporting Group and breed victories to his credit. Unfortunately, photos of him are not available as they were lost when the Washingtons' home was destroyed by fire in 1971. But his Best in Show wins were noted in Porter's record book at the kennel. Waarborg was Best in Show at BOTH Dallas and Ft. Worth two years in a row, a feat not yet repeated by any dog, and in addition to his all-breed successes had several Kees Specialty Shows to his credit.

Ch. Flakkee Instant Replay has 221 Bests of Breed to his credit, plus 146 Group and 45 times Best in Show.

The list of the Flakkee stud dogs and their famous offspring which follows is one which we feel should prove of interest and value to our readers. It was prepared for us by Mr. Washington.

Eng., Am. and Can. Ch. Wrocky of Wistonia*
Ch. Winston of Wistonia
Ch. Flakkee Wrockslide
Ch. Flakkee Wrock and Wroll
Ch. Flakkee Shamwrock
Ch. Flakkee Wrock Crystal
Ch. Cornelius Wrocky Selznick
Ch. Flakkee Wrococo
Ch. Ajkeers Wil-Wrock-Kim
Ch. Flakkee Wrock and Rye
Ch. Commander Coal of Fairville

Ch. Flakkee Fire Ball
Ch. Flakkee Firechief

Ch. Flakkee Silent Sentry
Ch. Lady Kay of Rocky Falls

Flakkee Fabian
Ch. Von Teufel

Ch. Lucifer's Imp of Hellzafire
Ch. Flakkee Inferno

Eng. and Am. Ch. Wilco of Wistonia
Eng., Am. and Can. Ch. Wrocky of Wistonia
Ch. Flakkee Favorite
Ch. Flakkee Fire Ball
Ch. Flakkee Flame
Ch. Flakkee Boss Man
Ch. Col. Applejack of Carmel
Ch. Ajkeer Pagan Magic
Ch. Rhapsody of Westcrest
Ch. Ruttkay Bell of Westcrest
Ch. Vibrato of Westcrest

Ch. Jee Jacs Mischief Maker
Ch. Maestro of Westcrest
Ch. Ajkeer Magic Hapi Ladd II

Ch. Flakkee Sweepstakes*
Ch. Flakkee Sky Wrocket
Ch. Flakkee Fresca Van Heusen
Ch. Stetler's Derby Stakes
Ch. Cinderella
Ch. Lottery
Ch. Belvedere Graf Arco
Ch. Fritz Van Vornaam C.D.X.
Ch. Hans van Voornaam
Ch. Stetler's Country Stakes
Ch. Keno of Heldervale
Ch. Flakkee Pit Boss
Ch. Flakkee Copasetic

Ch. Patriot Van Fitz
Ch. Flakkee Cover Girl
Ch. Flakkee Dusky Devil

Eng. and Am. Ch. Waarborg of Wistonia
Ch. Flakkee Free Lancer
Ch. Reeder's Thunderbolt
Ch. Ajkeer Kontiki
Ch. Onszuider Zee
Ch. Ajkeer Belita
Ch. Ons Zeekapitein
Ch. Taylor's Dutch Boy
Ch. Flakkee Fanfare of Van Bie
Ch. Erika of Warheid

Ch. Flakkee Dusky Devil*
Ch. Flakkee Silent Sentry
Ch. Flakkee Legend
Ch. Flakkee Fantasy

63

Ch. Flakkee Winsome Lass
Ch. Flakkee Dark Rascal

Ch. Flakkee Legend
Ch. Taylor's Jack of San Lin
Ch. Taylor's Cupid of San Lin

Flakkee Stud Poker
Ch. Hans Vegas

Ch. Worrall of Wistonia*
Ch. Flakkee Missouri Gambler
Ch. Flakkee Winsomemiss
Ch. Flakkee Jackpot
Ch. Flakkee Go Devil

Ch. Wistonia Aristocrat of Doral
Ch. Worrall of Wistonia
Ch. Flakkee Baronessa
Ch. Flakkee Countessa
Ch. Flakkee Diplomat
Ch. Flakkee Playmate

Ch. Cornelius Wrocky Selznick*
Ch. Flakkee Dynamite
Ch. Flakkee Sweepstakes
Ch. Lucifer's Imp of Helzafire
Ch. The Mews Autumn In Haze
Ch. Merrikee Wrocky Pooh Bear
Ch. Merrikee Wrocky Tip Topper,
C.D.
Ch. The Mews Monogram In Mist
Ch. Flakkee Wrockhound
Ch. Plantation Wrockaway
Ch. Van Heusen Wendy
Ch. Merrikkee Wrocky Monarch
O'Mischief
Ch. Merrikee Wrocky Royal Rogue
Ch. Merrikee Wrocky's Gay Minx

Ch. Wrockhound
Ch. Ajkeer Cholomay
Ch. Tryons Wrocken Robin

Ch. Tyrons Wrocky Road
Ch. Tryons Wrock Festival

Ch. Flakkee Instant Replay
Ch. Flakkee Duplicate
Ch. Tryons Instant Love
Ch. Flakkee Playback "76"
Ch. Flakkee Instamatic "77"
Ch. Chasen's Instant Pride and Joy
Ch. Flakkee Hasty Rhythm
Ch. Flakkee Moon Glow
Ch. Flakkee Shadow of the Desert
Ch. Flakkee Spitfire
Ch. Saint George
Ch. Silver Frost Bonanza

Ch. Flakkee Jackpot
Ch. Choice For Tryon
Ch. Star Kees Batman
Ch. Instant Replay
Ch. Merikee Sunny Debutante
Ch. Merikee Sunny Heritage
Ch. Windrift Midnite Masquerade
Ch. Merikee Legend of Worrall
Ch. Flakkee Jack Daniels
Ch. Flakkee Jack In The Box
Ch. Fearless Flashback
Ch. High Roller
Ch. Gangbusters
Ch. Import
Ch. Diamond Lil
Ch. Blackjack (Windrift's)
Ch Baronwood Calculated Risk
"76"
Ch. Silver Frost Huggy Bear
Ch. Sassy Miss D
Ch. Baronwood Guestimate
Ch. Flakkee Hijack
Ch. Keexote's Hi-Jacs of Modesto
Ch. Flakkee Jack Frost
Ch. Pickvale Jim Dandy
Ch. Flakkee Lil' Drummer Boy
Ch. Vanessa Von Jackpot

Ch. Flakkee Instamatic, America's Top Winning Kees during every year shown, 1977, 1978 and 1980. Six Bests in Show, 29 Groups, and 89 Best of Breeds stand on his record. Flakkee Kennels, Mr. and Mrs. Porter Washington, Lawndale, California.

Ch. Flakkee Instamatic
  Ch. Flakkee Vonryan's Express
  Ch. Flakkee Pride 'N Promise
  Ch. Vonryan's Ragamuffin
  Ch. Flakkee Fast Draw (B.I.S. Winner)
  Ch. Flakkee Taki of Vredendal
  Ch. Flakkee Knockout

  Ch. Flakkee Snapshot
  Ch. Vonryan's Jiffy James
  Ch. Flakkee Showdown

Ch. Flakkee Hijack
  Ch. Flakke Hijinx

Ch. Flakkee Knockout
  Ch. Flakkee Main Event

A lady and her dog!—the dearly loved Ch. Misty Lady of Kishamo was Mary Alice Smiley's gift to her mother.

Geronimo

Geronimo Keeshonden were established during the late 1960s by William and Mary Alice Smiley at Midland, Michigan.

Their first Keeshond was American and Canadian Champion Greheim's Geronimo (Champion Charles von Klompen—Greheim's Lady Charlene), who was primarily of Coventry and Keedox breeding, both lines tracing their way back to Wistonia. A Coventry-bred bitch bred to Geronimo produced the Smileys' lovely Champion Misty Lady of Kishamo, who in two litters produced half a dozen

Am. and Can. Ch. Greheim's Geronimo, one of Mary Alice Smiley's famous winners, Geronimo Keeshonden, Midland, Michigan.

Geronimo Blue Line is one of the many fine winning Geronimo Keeshonden bred by Mary Alice Smiley of Midland, Michigan.

champions. Following her second litter, Misty went to live with Mary Alice's mother, who loves her dearly and was having a problem at the time making the Smileys feel that the arrangement would be a nice one for both parties concerned. It worked out well indeed, as Mary Alice's mother truly takes boundless joy and pleasure in the companionship which Misty provides.

For her first litter, Misty had been bred to American and Canadian Champion Mar-I-Ben Hobgoblin, an outstanding dog whom the Smileys had purchased from Eloise Geiger of Canton, Ohio. The six puppies produced included four champions. Next time around, the stud selected for her was Champion Denwood's Gurney Halleck, and in this case there were two champions in four puppies added to her list.

The next bitch purchased by the Smileys was Loosenort's Alia of Denwood, she from a Keedox dam and sired by a son of the famed Champion Rich-Bob's Stormy Weather. Alia was bred to American and Canadian Champion Greheim's Geronimo, producing two champions from a total of six puppies. Then for her following litter, Champion Keedox Strawberry Shortcake was selected to be the sire. That added two more champions already finished and two others which, although sold as pets, are pointed. One of the daughters, kept by the Smileys, finished at thirteen months and has since produced dogs who are headed for the title.

The third and last time that Alia was bred it was to American and Canadian Champion Mar-I-Ben Hobgoblin, which worked out especially well resulting in two finished champions and two pointed dogs. One of the latter is particularly outstanding and a dog of which Mrs. Smiley expects big things when he comes into mature coat.

The Smileys can well take pride in having had fourteen champions in the sixteen years of owning Kees, with certainly many more in their future. What to them means far more than the show ring honors, however, is the fact that they are breeding dogs who combine soundness with beauty; and that these dogs are carrying on the wonderful "Geronimo" disposition—not in the least high-strung, but outgoing and friendly without being obnoxious.

Am. and Can. Ch. Geronimo's Hob-Bit, by Am. and Can. Ch. Mar-I-Ben Hobgoblin ex Ch. Misty Lady of Kishamo. Drawing by owner, Mary Alice Smiley, Geronimo Kennels, Midland, Michigan.

GreenKees

The GreenKees Keeshonden are owned by Mr. and Mrs. William (Bill and Tess) Eckhart at Greenland, New Hampshire, where some truly outstanding Kees representing England's finest bloodlines are to be found in a small but very select group of dogs.

Champion Ledwell Hyperion was the first Kees owned by the Eckharts, imported from Mrs. Scroggs' famed Ledwell Kennel in England, where so many exceptional Kees have been produced. This handsome dog, by English Champion Surprise of Ven ex English Champion Ledwell Charlotte, quickly made his presence felt on the American show scene under L. Mae Evans' handling, bringing many honors to his owners. Mrs. Eckhart remarks that "Jock loved his cup of tea and had one daily," in keeping with his English upbringing.

Ch. Ledwell Hyperion pictured here with his handler in the United States, L. Mae Evans, who piloted him, among other victories, to Winners Dog for a five-point "major" at the Keeshond Club of Delaware Valley's Lehigh Specialty.

Am. and Can. Ch. GreenKees Beowulf v Ledwell, by Eng. Ch. Ledwell Kardos ex Pure Honey of Ledwell, has had an exciting show career in the United States (handled by L. Mae Evans) and in Canada (handled by John Heartz). One of the famous Kees from GreenKees Kennels of Mr. and Mrs. William Eckhart, Greenland, New Hampshire.

Champion Rhinevale Ribstonpippin ("there will never be another Pippin" comments his owner) at ten years of age still has a sparkle in his eyes and is looking fit and handsome. Mrs. Eckhart remarks upon his strong resemblance to English Champion Riesling of Rhinevale. Pippin was the 1975 Top Winning Kees owned by a member of the Heritage Trail Keeshond Club. He is a son of the great English Champion Ledwell Dutchman (winner of 25 British Challenge Certificates) ex English Champion Raffetta of Rhinevale.

American and Canadian Champion GreenKees Beowulf V. Ledwell is a son of English Champion Ledwell Kardos ex Pure Honey of Ledwell, the latter a Dutchman daughter ex Quinta of Ven, she by English Champion Surprise of Ven from English Champion Viviandiere of Ven. "Bear" was # 5 Keeshond Club of America Dog for 1982, despite the fact that he was shown during only eight months of that year. Additionally, he also won the Heritage Trail Keeshond Club Award for top member-owned dog that year.

Champion GreenKees Kismmet V. Ledwell is a sister to Beowulf, and is now retired. She is a bitch of lovely coloring with correct dark eyes and did well during her show career handled by L. Mae Evans.

The lovely young dog, Champion GreenKees Pipson Caesar, is a very handsome example of correct Keeshond quality and type. He completed his title when only twenty months of age at the Capital

Ch. GreenKees Pipson Caesar is a beautiful example of the quality Kees to be found at the Eckharts' GreenKees Kennels in Greenland, New Hampshire. This lovely dog completed his title at the Capital Keeshond Specialty at 20 months of age by going Winners Dog and Best of Winners. Handled by L. Mae Evans.

Keeshond Specialty where he went Best of Winners. His admirers are many.

Then there is the exquisite bitch, Champion Ledwell Britannia, by English and American Champion Keesland Fisherman ex Ledwell Quetta, who was never out of the ribbons en route to her title, completing her championship within an eight-week period of time. She was bred by Mrs. Sylvia Scroggs in England, and is a most gorgeous example of what to look for in a truly quality Kees bitch!

Tess and Bill Eckhart are dedicated workers for the good of their breed, who have given much time, thought, and energy to keeping and improving upon the quality of their dogs. We would say that they are succeeding admirably!

Kenarae

Kenarae Keeshond Kennels are owned by Ken and Nancy Springer at Sellers, South Carolina, who started showing their first Kees in 1972, Champion Mist of Spring, who is now thirteen years old. Since that time they have gained championships with eight of their Keeshonden.

After the first several years of showing, the Springers decided that they wanted to start breeding. A good deal of advance study went into selection of the bloodlines with which they would work, the final decision being that they liked the imports, English and American Champion Dalbaro Beachcomber and English and American Champion Raccassius of Rhinevale. Thus they acquired Champion Damarkee The Party Crasher, a Beachcomber son; and Champion Keeszar Mint Julep v Kenarae, a Rhinevale granddaughter.

Champion Damarkee The Party Crasher, "Bogart" to his friends, completed his championship and went on to win Best in Show on the

Ch. Keeszar Mint Julep v Kenarae belongs to Kenarae Kees, Ken and Nancy Springer, Sellers, South Carolina.

Ch. Kenarae Beauchamp's Six Pak belongs to Ken and Nancy Springer, Sellers, South Carolina.

same day in 1977. He had several Group placements and another Best in Show before retiring after a two-year show career. He was # 7 Kees, *Kennel Review* System, in 1977 and # 6 in 1978. "Bogart" has sired eight champions, several sons that are major pointed (undoubtedly finished by now) and has at least several champion grandchildren.

The Springers' first breeding between "Bogart" and Julie, their Rhinevale bitch, produced seven boys and one girl in the litter: Six of these puppies became champions as follows:

1) The bitch, Champion Kenarae Pat'N Pending, was # 4 bitch, *Keezette* System, in 1979. She won Best of Opposite Sex at the Capital Keeshond Club Specialty at the age of ten months, and had many Bests of Breed over "specials" from the puppy class. She was beginning her "specials" career as we were gathering material for this book after raising her first litter of puppies, ten months old at that time.

2) Champion Kenarae Beauchamp's Six Pak, out as a "special" has done well with Group placements, including a Group 3rd at only eight months old.

3) Champion Kenarae The Silver Streak also has won several Group placements.

4) Champion Kenarae Silver Edition is a Specialty winner.

5) Champion Nautica's Kenarae Dark Dream is a Group 1 winner.

The Springers are justly proud of the success with which their Kees are meeting. For three consecutive years, 1976 through 1978, they won the top winning dog award from the Capital Keeshond Club, and retired the Mar-I-Ben Challenge Trophy.

Ch. Kenarae Pat'N Pending, owned by Ken and Nancy Springer, Kenarae Keeshonden, Sellers, South Carolina.

Ch. Kenarae The Silver Streak, owned by Ken and Nancy Springer, Kenarae Keeshonden, Sellers, South Carolina.

Lupini

Lupini Keeshonden, at Big Rock, Illinois, are owned by Joan and A.R. Magliozzi, and closely line-bred on Champion Rich-Bob's Stormy Weather, ROMX and Champion Flakkee Jackpot, ROMX, primarily through Champion Star-Kees Batman, ROMX, which limits it to being mainly the old Wistonia line with a bit of Ruttkay.

The Magliozzis' foundation bitch is Champion Gregory's Pittance of Tryon, ROM, a daughter of Gregory's Zilver Vox from American and Canadian Champion Tryon's Tuppence, Tuppence being the litter sister to Champion Tryon's Fearless Fruhling, ROMX, Top Producing Kees Bitch in the History of the Breed. Bred by Donald R. Gregory, Pittance has scored in the show ring and as a producer, having won consistently, including Best of Opposite Sex at the first Keeshond Fanciers of Central States Specialty in 1977. She is the dam, in her only litter, of five champions sired by Champion Windrift's Lover Boy, all of which finished with distinction, not just perseverance. These include Champion Lupini Pretty Boy Floyd, who finished in August 1981 with three "majors" and Best of Breed over some leading "specials" en route to the title; Best in Sweepstakes at the Sahuaro Specialty; and he also did well at the National in conjunction with which it was held. Now he is watching his own progeny, as he has a champion already in his first litter (at a year old) and two others pointed as we write.

Littermate to Floyd, Champion Lupini Lovely Weather finished with a 4-point "major" and Best of Breed from the classes at the Chicago-International in 1981, has had numerous breed wins since then, was Best of Opposite Sex at the Keeshond Fanciers of Central States 1980 Specialty, and Best of Opposite Sex at the Heart of America Keeshond Specialty in 1982. Dam of one litter of three, the male has six Canadian points as of December 1983, and a female is already a breed winner from the classes.

Littermate Champion Lupini Mobs Moll, owned by William and Carolyn Coughlin, finished in October 1981, taking Winners Bitch at the Sahuaro Keeshond Specialty on the way. Another of these puppies, Champion Lupini Hit Man, owned by George and Janet Hill, finished in nine shows with four consecutive "majors." The fifth of them, Champion Sir Rank's Dwarrelwind Lupini, owned by Tom and Bonnie Rank, was shown only twice as a puppy, but when she started serious campaigning, in June 1982, she finished with eight con-

Ch. Lupini Pretty Boy Floyd, homebred dog owned by A.R. and Joan Magliozzi, winning Best of Breed at Cedar Rapids in June 1982.

Ch. Lupini Lovely Weather, by Ch. Windrift's Lover Boy ex Ch. Gregory's Pittance of Tryon, ROM. Pictured here going Best of Winners at the Heart of America Kees Specialty in 1982. A homebred owned by Joan & Dick Magliozzi, Big Rock, Illinois.

FOURTH IN GROUP
BURLINGTON · K.C.
AUGUST 21, 1982
OLSON PHOTO

Ch. Playmate Tic Tac of Toes, by Ch. Grawyn's Klassic Kasanova ex Am. and Can. Ch. Tryon's Tuppence was bred by Donald R. Gregory and is owned by Joan F. and A.R. Magliozzi, Lupini Kennels, Big Rock, Illinois.

secutive wins. A sixth from this litter may well be finished, too, by the time you are reading this as Lupini Enforcer has "major" points although shown very sparingly. All of the foregoing are from Pittance's one litter of nine. Pretty Boy, Lovely Weather and Enforcer are all breeder-owned by the Magliozzis.

Joan and Dick Magliozzi also are owners of the smashing young dog Champion Playmate Tic Tac of Toes, by Champion Graywyn's Klassic Kasanove ex American and Canadian Champion Tryon's Tuppance, 4★ Dam. This handsome dog was Best in Sweepstakes at the 1980 Keeshond Fanciers of Central States, and finished in March 1981. A multiple Breed winner and consistent Group placer in limited showing, he is a double grandson of Champion Rich-Rob's Stormy Weather, ROMX. A daughter from his first litter went Winners Bitch and Best of Winners at the 1982 So-Cal Specialty from the 9-12 months puppy class, and placed the other day, finishing quite easily before two years of age. From Tic Tac's next three litters, with a total of twelve puppies all at or under a year's age, he has one with six Canadian points and a Best Puppy in Group (from Champion Lupini Lovely Weather), two breed winners, three with "major" points, and a total of eight so far with points out of the twelve, two of which have not as yet been shown.

Tic Tac's litter brother, Champion Playmate Lone Ranger finished with three "majors" including Winners Dog at the Keeshond Club of Delaware Valley Specialty, and the other litter brother also is "major" pointed.

Joan Magliozzi feels that her best litter to date has been the one sired by Champion Windrift's Lover Boy from Champion Gregory's Pittance of Tryon. Les Baker owns Lover Boy, bred by Joanne Sanford

Ch. Gregory's Pittance of Tryon, ROM, by Gregory's Zilver Vox ex Am. and Can. Ch. Tryon's Tuppence, was bred by Donald R. Gregory and is owned by Joan F. Magliozzi at Lupini Kennels.

Reed, and he is from an all-champion litter, a breeding which, repeated again, produced an all champion litter. His litter sister is Champion Windrift's Love Unlimited, HOF, and his full brother is Champion Windrift's Fair 'n' Square. A full sister, Champion Windrift's Hollywood Squares, is the dam of the Best in Show Champion Windrift's Gambler, C.D., HOF. Mrs. Magliozzi's success in using this dog on her excellent bitches, which resulted in the five champions in Pittance's litter followed by the outstanding litter from Tuppence, places emphasis on the importance of breeding from strong PRODUCING bloodlines! It is interesting to note that the litter by Lover Boy from Champion Tryon's Tuppence (who is the dam of Pittance and of Tic Tac of Toes) produced the Winners Bitch at the Keeshond Fanciers of Central States Specialty in 1981, Champion Playmate Lullaby, who finished in five shows from the 6-9 month puppy class, now has her C.D., plus breed wins to her credit. One of her littermates is also "major" pointed; another will be entering the ring shortly.

The Magliozzis would certainly seem to have struck the perfect breeding combination for their dogs, and we look upon their success with admiration.

Moonshadow

Moonshadow Kees are owned by Tom and Ellen Crewe at Green Bay, Wisconsin, and the interest here is in both obedience and show competition.

The star of this kennel is Canadian Champion and Obedience Trial Champion Tigger's Moonshadow, Canadian and American U.D., the third Kees in history to have garnered all these obedience degrees, and only the second to be, as well, a conformation champion. The story of Tigger's obedience career is told in the obedience section of this book.

Tigger is of Wistonia and Coventry descent, by Mayo Supreme from Sirocco's Glory. He was born September 18th 1974, bred by Clifton H. Toenges. He was five years old when Ellen Crewe decided to take him to obedience school and, despite warnings that "he would never earn a degree because of his age" Ellen and Tigger achieved a memorable record.

Ellen had shown Tigger only a couple of times in the breed prior to December 1981, during which he had taken all reserves, but always over real competition. Then one day at a supported entry (Specialty) in Toronto he won not only the second leg on his C.D.X., but also took Best of Winners for a 3-point "major" despite his by then age of seven

Mutual admiration between "Tigger" and his trainer/handler/co-owner Ellen Crewe is very obvious in this picture. Can. Ch. and O.T. Ch. Tigger's Moonshadow, Am. and Can. U.D. is owned by Tom and Ellen Crewe, Green Bay, Wisconsin.

years and three months! Being almost a third of the way towards his Canadian championship, and with Canada so short a trip from their home in Wisconsin, was more than Ellen could resist, so whenever they infrequently went to Canada for any purpose, Ellen entered him and he never let her down. At all but one show he competed in both conformation and obedience, and most of the time he was successful in both rings on the same day. He completed his championship on September 16th 1983 by taking Winners dog, Best of Winners and Best of Breed over a Group winning "special" AND took fourth place in a large Utility Class with a 187½ "just for fun"—two days before his ninth birthday.

Ellen Crewe hopes that her experiences with Tigger may encourage owners of other Keeshonden to explore the potential in their dogs, adding that "a dog is never too old to learn, and obedience work especially is extremely beneficial to both a Kees and his owner. The level of communication that develops during those training sessions is incredible. No one has ever guessed Tigger's age correctly and I can't help but think that the Obedience training has played a major role in keeping my 'grand old man' looking and acting like a youngster."

Possum Trot

Possum Trot Keeshonden were established in the early 1960s by Mrs. Zoe Bemis at Bryn Mawr, Pennsylvania, who has worked principally since the very beginning with the Wistonia bloodlines. Her first purchase, Champion Shaywood Toreador, was from Wistonia; and the most recent young hopeful, as this is written, is Wistonia Windham, by Champion Willy Weaver of Wistonia ex Champion Wistonia Wyndixie.

Winning Kees owned by Mrs. Bemis over the years, many of them shown by her daughter Charlotte (Toni) White (who is married to noted Beagle breeder and judge, John D. White, Jr.), include Possum Trot Charisma and Champion Possum Trot Meena, both from the 1970s. Also there have been Champion Saints Retreats Wromulus, Champion Rockhold Frolic of Ramsgate, Shady Hill's Harum Scarum, and, owned by Toni and Jack White, Champion Ramsgate Little Knight.

Possum Trot Charisma at the Keeshond Club of America Specialty in April 1970. Owned and handled by Mrs. Zoe W. Bemis.

Ch. Shaywood Toreador, from Wistonia Kennels in England, was the first Kees owned by Zoe W. Bemis and her daughter Charlotte White. Shown extensively and successfully by Charlotte White during the 1960s. Toreador is also owned by J.B. Mitchell.

Shady Hill's Harum Scarum taking the breed at Charlottesville-Albemarle in 1981. Co-owned by Mrs. Zoe W. Bemis and her daughter Mrs. Charlotte White.

Ruttkay

Ruttkay Kennels were begun in Winchester, Virginia, in 1946 by the late Mrs. Virginia Ruttkay who passed away in August of 1982. A major portion of today's Kees kennels have Ruttkay stock in the ancestry of their dogs. L. Mae Evans, Kees breeder and professional handler who was a good friend of Mrs. Ruttkay's, along with "a loosely formed corporation of Ruttkay advocates, pooling such resources as puppy placement, breeding stock, handling service, pedigree service, new owner orientation, displaced dog referral, dog placement assurance resulting from owner death or disability," to quote Mae Evans, are carrying on the Ruttkay line, and it is to her that we are indebted for the information from which this Ruttkay resume has been compiled.

Mrs. Ruttkay was among the country's pioneer breeders of Keeshonden, and worked consistently for the breed's advancement through her positions as an early Board member of the Keeshond Club of America and as a charter member of the Keeshond Club of Delaware Valley. She gained wide promotion for the Keeshond breed with publicity on it in television, radio, newspapers, as well as by many excellent and informative articles on the breed in *Popular Dogs* and *Dog World* (which spanned a period of many years) and others.

The Ruttkay Keeshonden were founded on Ruttkay Skyrocket, Champion Brielle of Remlewood, American and Canadian Champion Conwood Kloos, Conwood Gilda, Ruttkay Conwood Hildegarde, Ruttkay Romance, and Champion Ruttkay Evening Star. In the mid-1950s Mrs. Ruttkay moved her kennel from Virginia to Royersford, Pennsylvania. The foundation stock and genetic additions were based on English stock of *early* Dutch *origin*. These included Van Zaandam—(Mrs. Digby, England), Vorden—(Mrs. Tucker, England), Guelder—(Mrs. Gatacre, Holland and England), and Evenlode—(Miss Hastings, England).

Successful early imports to Ruttkay included Canadian and American Champion Sinterklaas Brave Nimrod, ROMX; Irish and American Champion Karel of Altnavanog, ROM; Canadian and American Champion Conwood Kloos; Tenby Tina and Conwood Gilda. Successful American-bred foundation and/or infusions include Champion Ruttkay Roem, ROMX; Champion Maverick Son of Ilka; Park Cliffe Mia Van Pelt; Ruttkay Jezro's Gay Nathalia, ROM; Ruttkay Conwood Hildegarde; Ruttkay Numi of Frostridge; Champion

Ch. Karel of Altnavanog, ROM, by Eng. Ch. Verschansing of Vorden ex Irish Ch. Khristine of Seafield. Ruttkay Kennels, photo courtesy of L. Mae Evans.

Ruttkay Go Go Girl of Modesto; Champion Brielle of Remlewood; and Ruttkay Callie of Modesto.

It is interesting to note that most of the above have produced nine to fourteen generations of progeny!

Later importations included some who were Dutch and some from Germany, none of which contributed successfully to the desired type, and thus were discontinued.

Impressive indeed is the fact that there are more than two hundred champions on record with BOTH Ruttkay sire and dam; and more than one hundred with *either* a Ruttkay sire *or* dam, which we understand from Mae Evans as of January 1983 represents more than ten per cent of ALL Keeshonden bearing American championship titles! Additionally, 22 Ruttkay Kees have earned foreign titles, these in England, Mexico, Canada, Ireland, the Dominican Republic and Ecuador, and the only Cuban champion in the breed.

Am. and Can. Ch. Sinterklaas Brave Nimrod, ROMX *26, by Eng. Ch. Big Bang of Evenlode *9 ex Sinterklaas Lass of Vankeena. Photo courtesy of L. Mae Evans.

Ruttkay Keeshonden have won a total of seven Bests in Show, these honors having been gained by Champion Ruttkay Heir Apparent (one), Champion De Vignon's Ducomo (three), Champion Ruttkay Sirius (two) and Champion Ruttkay Commander (one).

Champion Ruttkay Sirius, Champion Ruttkay Commander, Champion Jul-Day Wunderlust de Sylvia, Champion De Vignon's Ducomo, Champion Ruttkay Clyde's Cubby, Champion Rovic's Chimney Blaze, U.D., and Champion Van Mell's Pot of Gold are all in the Hall of Fame. Eight of the Ruttkay dogs are in the Register of Merit: Irish and American Champion Karel of Altnavanog (twelve champions produced), Champion Ruttkay Zilver Frost Van Roem (six champions), Ruttkay Jezro's Gay Nathalia (five champions), Ruttkay Tricia of Kathrdon (seven champions), Champion Lorelei Van Ruttkay (five champions), Champion Ruttkay Go Man Go (twelve champions), Champion Ruttkay Bold Venture (thirteen champions), and Champion Keli-Kees Erin O'Mist (five champions).

Then three have the distinguished title "Register of Merit Excellent": Champion Ruttkay Little Miss Napua (dam of eight champions), Champion Sinterklaas Brave Nimrod (sire of 26 champions), and Champion Ruttkay Roem, sire of 33 champions who received the Irene Schlintz Showdog Top Producer Award.

Ch. Ruttkay Clyde's Cubby, by Ch. Maverick Son of Ilka ex Ch. Ruttkay Misty Morning, another splendid example of the superb Kees raised at Ruttkay Kennels. Photo courtesy of L. Mae Evans.

Ch. Ruttkay Heir Apparent, by Irish and Am. Ch. Karel of Altnavanog ROM *12 ex Ruttkay Romance. Photo courtesy of L. Mae Evans.

Among the Ruttkay best in Specialty Show winners have been Ch. Ruttkay Sirius, Champion Ruttkay Clyde's Cubby, Champion Maverick Son of Ilka, and Champion Ruttkay Commander. But this list is far from complete.

Mrs. Ruttkay was an interested participant in obedience competition, too, and at least 82 dogs from Ruttkay have C.D. titles (there are 31 with both Champion and Companion Dog honors), 23 are C.D.X. (eight of whom are also conformation champions), four are Utility Dogs, of which three also have conformation titles, and there is a Tracking Dog.

Nine of the first fifteen O.F.A. Certified Keeshonden in the United States were of Ruttkay breeding.

The only American-bred Keeshond ever imported to England as this book is written was Champion Ruttkay Moerdaag of Ven. He did well for the breed there, and won the Razor Cup Award for sire of greatest number of class winning get in a Keeshond Club of England Specialty, which honor he gained in 1966.

Typical Ruttkay puppies: *(Left to right)* Ruttkay Roly Poly Dutch Girl, Ruttkay Roem, and Ruttkay Reuzenwerk, all by Ch. Van Ons Furious ex Ch. Ruttkay Muundawg.

Ch. Dean's Shirtrai Jit Jot Roc, by Ch. Silva Thunder-on Van Rijn Aak ex Ch. Nordeen's Silver Keya Von Aak, C.D., pictured winning the Heart of America Keeshond Specialty 1975 under the very famous Keeshond breeder Mrs. Clementine Peterson who is judging. Shirley Trainer, owner.

Shirtrai

Tom and Shirley Trainer, owners of the Shirtrai Kennels at Oskaloosa, Iowa, share their dog interests and activities between Keeshonden and Black and Tan Coonhounds, very successfully in both cases.

So far as the Kees are concerned, we note Shirley and some very splendid dogs in the winners circle back in the early 1970s, consistently and continuing to the present.

89

Champion Shirtrai Jit Jot Rocket, bred by Mr. and Mrs. J.M. De Groot, was Best of Opposite Sex to the Grand Sweepstakes Winner at the Heart of America Keeshond Club specialty in 1973. Sired by Champion Dean's Shirtrai Jit Jot Roc ex Smokey's Queen of Columbia.

Champion Shirtrai Puf 'N Stuf won the Sweepstakes of the Heart of America Specialty in 1974, this one by Champion Markitz Speculation ex Nordeen's Invincible Girl, bred by Velva Bell Nordeen.

Champion Dean's Shirtrai Jit Jot Roc (Champion Silva Thunder-on Van Rijn Aak ex Champion Nordeen's Silver Kaya Von Aak, C.D.), won the American Keeshond Club National Specialty in 1975, a singular honor since the judge was that very great authority on this breed, Mrs. Clementine Peterson.

The current "young hopeful" as we write this in 1983 is Champion Shirtrai Mystic Playboy, by Champion Dean's Jit Jot Roc ex Champion Nordeen's Baroness De Groot, who in September of this year took Best of Breed at the Specialty of the Central States Keeshond Club.

Shirley Trainer remarks that while "all wins are fun, those at Specialties are extra so." Surely she must be gratified, feeling this way, at the consistency with which her dogs have made their presence felt in keenest competition at these events!

Ch. Shirtrai's Mystic Playboy in February 1983 winning the Non-Sporting Group at southeastern Iowa. Owned by Shirley Trainer, Oskaloosa, Iowa.

A lovely study of Sonja Sobaka of Holloridge, ROM, by Flakkee Wrockus of Erie ex Kenmerk Precious Panda, foundation bitch at Patricia Katomski-Beck's Sobaka Kennels, Plattsmouth, Nebraska.

Sobaka

Sobaka Kennels, located at Plattsmouth, Nebraska, belong to Patricia Katomski-Beck, who describes herself as a "misplaced Connecticut Yankee" having been born and raised in New Britain, Connecticut. Pat can surely well survey with pride her success in the Keeshond world as since 1978 Sobaka-bred Kees have finished eight American championships, eight Canadian championships, six American C.D. Degrees, and three Canadian C.D. Degrees. Which is very nice going any way one looks at it!

Sonja Sobaka of Holloridge, ROM, by Flakkee Wrockus of Erie ex Kenmerk Precious Panda, was bred by D. Holloway. She was, in May 1983, awarded the title of ROM (Registry of Merit) as the dam of five American champions. The Keeshond Club of Canada awarded her "Outstanding Brood Bitch" in 1983 for being the dam of three Canadian champions. At the 1980 Keeshond Club of America National Specialty she won the Brood Bitch Class.

Sonja was the foundation bitch at Sobaka, and died in September 1982 at eleven years of age.

Among Sonja's well-known progeny are the following:

American and Canadian Champion Sobaka's Steppenralf, America and Canadian C.D. (by Champion Jappie de Eerste), who is the sire of a Canadian champion and numerous pointed offspring. He is a multiple breed winner in both the United States and Canada.

American and Canadian Champion Call me Leon T. Sobaka, American and Canadian C.D., (also by Champion Jappie de Eerste), who finished in the United States at one year and nineteen days of age with five "majors." He is a multiple Best of Breed winner in the United States and Canada and has Group placements in both countries at less than two years old.

American and Canadian Champion Eleanora B. Sobaka, a littermate to Ralf.

American and Canadian Champion Sobaka Charlie's Angel (by Champion Keli-Kees Replica of Roddy), a multiple Best of Breed winner in the United States. "Farrah" is the dam of two American champions and three Canadian champions, plus other pointed offspring and an American champion granddaughter. She finished her Canadian championship in four consecutive shows.

American and Canadian Champion Sobaka Rodean Ado Annie, American and Canadian C.D., by Champion Keli-Kees Replica of Roddy, the dam of a champion, and well started on a good career in obedience.

Tanglewood

Tanglewood Keeshonden were established by Carol J. Aubut of Westford, Massachusetts, in 1956, although her actual breeding program did not get under way until 1960. Her first Keeshond was Nether-Lair's Jon V. Tanglewood, who was a birthday present to her from the Cowleys, owners of Nether-Lair Kennels. After having this dog for a very short time, Carol knew that this was the breed for her, and it has been now for the past 22 years.

Carol later bought a bitch from Keeshof Kennels in Connecticut who was to become Champion Bright Promise of Keeshof. She had only two litters of puppies, then had to be spayed. From the same kennel, Carol's next two acquisitions were selected, both very outstanding males: Champion Herzog V Herman of Keeshof and Champion Bingo van Kogi of Keeshof. Both of these dogs were excellent studs and were many times breed and Group winners.

Nether-Lair's Jon V. Tanglewood, Carol J. Aubut's first Keeshond, who "got the whole thing started" for her and for Tanglewood Kennels.

Champion Herzog became the foundation stud dog of the Tanglewood Kennels. He was born in 1965 and to this day his name still appears in most of Tanglewood pedigrees. His sire was the extremely famous Best in Show winner, Champion Nederlan Herman v Mack. His dam was a litter sister to Champion Bingo. All three of these dogs were the combination of Vorden (which was a famed English kennel) and leading American bloodlines.

Although Champion Herzog had his fair share of champion offspring, Carol found his grandchildren were better than his children. His show record was very impressive, and he had the honor of being # 5 Keeshond for 1969.

In the late 1960s and early 1970s breeding at Tanglewood was curtailed for a few years, but in 1975 Carol Aubut bred a bitch called Champion Tanglewood Too Much. This was a granddaughter of

Champion Herzog, and she was to have been Carol's foundation bitch until her untimely death by fire changed these plans, when she was only two years old. Although Carol did get one litter from her, it was not exactly the way she wanted to breed her; but she was thus able to retain the bloodlines.

In 1976 Tanglewood acquired and co-owned the very outstanding Champion Holland Hond's Landmark. He is the combination of Vorden, Dutch and American bloodlines, and he works in very well with the Champion Herzog granddaughters and great granddaughters. He is the sire of sixteen champions, he is in the Keeshond Hall of Fame, and he is an ROM (Register of Merit) dog. His show record speaks for itself, with 75 Bests of Breed, 34 Group placements, and six Group Firsts.

Ch. Tanglewood Too Much, granddaughter of Ch. Herzog, winning a good Group placement. Owned and handled by Carol J. Aubut, Westford, Massachusetts.

Ch. Tanglewood Miles Standish winning Best of Breed from the classes to finish his championship before his first birthday. Carol J. Aubut, breeder-handler, Westford, Massachusetts.

Tanglewood's latest "star" is the outstanding Champion Tanglewood Miles Standish, owned by Kioona Kennels in Cross River, New York. He is a combination of the entire Tanglewood breeding program, being a Champion Landmark grandson (out of a Champion Landmark daughter) and he is a great-great grandson of Champion Nederlan Herman v Mack on his sire's side and a great-great grandson of Champion Herzog. His show record in early 1983 stood at 28 Bests of Breed, nine Group placements, and two Group Firsts at the tender age of two years. All concerned with him have high hopes for this young dog, not only as a show dog but as a breeding animal as well. Puppies by him, of which we have heard good things, are coming along looking really splendid, and by now should be distinguishing themselves in the ring.

Over the years, Tanglewood has finished more than 30 champions. Carol Aubut takes particular pride in the fact that with very few variations the kennel has used and worked with the same bloodlines as those on which it was originally started more than twenty years ago.

Tryon

We are deeply indebted to Carolyn Wray, who describes herself as "one of the Ellis kids who used to hang around the show rings of the northwest" for her permission to bring you an outline, for which she has supplied the basic information, of the very magnificent Tryon Keeshonden, who were highly successful dogs themselves and who have contributed significantly to their breed, owned by her mother Jean Ellis.

The story of Tryon began back in the early 1950s when Jean Ellis owned, bred, and showed Smooth Dachshunds. Her aunt, Grace Taylor of Amarillo, Texas, actually introduced her to Kees through the purchase of one for herself, from the Porter Washingtons. This dog became Champion Flakkee Legend, C.D. and in the manner of the breed promptly won the hearts of friends and family. It was he who became the first Texas Kees to win a Group there and the first Kees in the state to gain a C.D. title. So pleased was Mrs. Taylor with this dog that she decided to have more, and so Flakkee Dutch Love was purchased from the Washingtons and a kennel name was selected, "Taylors of San Lin," the latter a combination of the names of her two daughters. Mrs. Taylor took several Kees to obedience titles (and a Pomeranian as well). Her death in 1978, on the weekend of the Keeshond Club of America National at Dallas, was a sad loss to the Kees world.

Jean Ellis spent many summers at her aunt's ranch on the outskirts of Amarillo, growing to increasingly admire her aunt's handsome and intelligent dogs. When the Ellis family moved from their former home to Oregon, where they found living much to their liking, one thing was missing, especially in the eyes of the kids—a dog! Of course a Kees was the chosen breed, and following a beginners class in obedience, the new acquisition, Little Brother Jantje, entered the Novice A class with the eldest of the Ellis girls, Jane. Two legs on his C.D., plus a "major" in conformation generated considerable excitement among the Ellis youngsters, and soon Carolyn, after attending a few shows as a spectator, wanted a dog of her own. So Jantje, by then sporting a C.D. title, was joined in December 1965, by a six-month-old puppy who became Lovely Lady of Voornaam, U.D.

It is only natural that Jean Ellis, who had already tasted the fun of dog show competition through her earlier Dachshunds, soon should be joining daughters Jane and Carolyn in the show ring, but now with

Am. and Can. Ch. Tryon's Tuppence. By Ch. Rich-Bob's Stormy Weather, ROMX, from Ch. Tryon's Pound Sterling, C.D., ROM. Breeder, Ellis and Haberman. Photo courtesy of Joan Magliozzi.

Am. and Can. Ch. Tryon's Coin of the Realm, by Ch. Star-Kee's Batman, ROMX, from Ch. Flakkee's Choice for Tryon, CDX, was a very special dog to the Ellis family at home as well as a highly successful winner. Jean Ellis, owner, Tryon Kennels, Oregon.

Family Portrait at Tryon: (From the left) Ch. Tryon's Coin of the Realm, Ch. Tryon's Pound Sterling, C.D.; Ch. Flakkee's Choice for Tryon, C.D.X.; Lovely Lady of Voornaam, U.D.; Ch. Fritz Van Voornaam, U.D., HOF. All owned by Jean Ellis of the noted Tryon Kennels in Oregon.

Am. and Can. Ch. Tryon's Pound Sterling, C.D., by Ch. Star-Kee's Batman, ROMX, from Ch. Flakkee's Choice For Tryon, C.D.X., owned by Jean Ellis, Tryon Kennels, Oregon.

a Kees. A promising puppy from Lady's litter by Jantje was the dog who brought her back into the ring, and that became the first of many champions for Tryon Keeshonden, appropriately named Tryon's First Try.

In 1968 Jean Ellis purchased a bitch puppy from Flakkee Kennels. This became Champion Flakkee's Choice for Tryon, C.D.X., who in her first show, at the age of thirteen months, won a "major" at Tacoma, Washington, in June 1969. Trained and handled by Carolyn, she earned her C.D., after which she returned to conformation competition and won her second "major," again at Tacoma, this time a year later, in June 1970, quickly completing her title within the next couple months.

Choice for Tryon ("Gypsy" to friends) was a daughter of Champion Flakkee Jackpot, ROMX, HOF. With the idea of doubling up on the outstanding head of Jackpot's sire, English, American, and Canadian Champion Wrocky of Wistonia, Jean Ellis chose a Wrocky son as the stud to whom she should be bred, the handsome young Champion Star-Kees Batman, ROMX.

American and Canadian Champion Tryon's Coin of the Realm and Champion Tryon's Pound Sterling, a dog and a bitch, were kept at "Tryon" from this litter. Both started gaining points from the puppy classes, and Pound Sterling was trained and taken most of the way to her C.D. by Carolyn. When this lovely bitch was ten months old, on one of her show appearances she attracted the attention of Andrea Haberman from Gig Harbor, Washington, basically at that time an Alaskan Malamute fancier who had lately succumbed to the charms of a Kees and purchased Van Order's Heidi Ho for obedience and as a family pet. Andrea Haberman loved Jean Ellis' pretty young bitch on sight, and they arranged a co-ownership by which Andrea took the bitch, completed her championship and raised three litters from her, Jean Ellis taking the best of the show prospect puppies to work with socializing and ring training. The program worked out well for both ladies, and enabled Jean to maintain a breeding program without trying the patience of the "non-doggy" part of her family.

Coin of the Realm, meanwhile, had become a special member of the Ellis household, while at the same time gaining his championship, shown mostly by his owner but occasionally by professional handler Ted Luke. This dog was a consistent winner both in the States and Canada although shown sparingly, and was successful as a stud dog as well. Champion Frostridge Here Comes the Sun and Champion

Frostridge Maggie Mae both were sired by him, bred by Gail Klein of New Mexico from her Ruttkay bitch. Also he was the sire of Cascadia Keeshonden's first litter which produced Cascadia Platinum Gypsy (dam of Batman's well-known daughter American and Canadian Champion Kagins Asmant Beau Jest) and Cascadia Stormy Cricket, C.D.

Others of note in the Batman-Choice for Tryon litter included Tryon's Double Eagle, who as a puppy had been sold to a college professor. Tryon's Double Eagle had points and a Best of Breed win but was only shown occasionally.

For her second litter, born in December 1972, Champion Flakkee's Choice for Tryon, C.D.X. was bred to Champion Flakkee Instant Replay, HOF, again a half brother. These "Instant" puppies included future Champion Tryon's Instant Love, Tryon's Instant Happiness, and Tryon's Instant Mischief, ROM, the latter becoming a highly successful and important producer who also had fourteen points towards championship. "Misty" was sold, following a couple of litters at "Tryon," to Julia Boylan for whom she promptly added three more champions to her list.

Choice for Tryon was spayed, after which she went to Carolyn Ellis Wray to complete her C.D.X. Always a housepet, Carolyn describes her as "the cornerstone of the Tryon Kees." Sad to say, she was killed after being hit by a car in January of 1977.

Champion Tryon's Pound Sterling, the lovely bitch from the Batman-Choice for Tryon litter, for her own first litter was bred to Champion Flakkee Wrockhound, a dog that Jean Ellis had "much admired." The offspring included Champion Tryon's Wrocky Road, Champion Tryon's Wrockin Robin, Champion Tryon's Wrock Festival, Tryon's Ms. Got Wrocks, ROM, and Canadian Champion Tryon's Little Wrock Riot, who had both "majors" and a Best Puppy in Specialty here in the United States. Wrock Festival and Ms. Got Wrocks were added to Judy Daugherty's breeding program, where they have produced seven champions.

Tryon's first outcross was in 1974, when Pound Sterling was bred to Champion Rich-Bob's Stormy Weather, ROMX. Carolyn says "Jean felt it would be a good breeding, and it was!" Two puppies comprised the litter, becoming Champion Tryon's Tuppence and Champion Tryon's Fearless Fruehling, ROMX, informally known as "Toes" and "T'Other." In three litters totalling nine puppies "Toes" has produced three champions. "T'Other" became the famed "Cookie

Monster," and is the TOP PRODUCING Kees bitch of all time with sixteen champions from the twenty-five puppies from three litters. She is the recipient of an Irene Schlintz Phillips System Gold Certificate for her producing record. The "Cookie Monster" completed her championship when only ten and a half months old, and was the Top Winning Member Owned Dog from the Keeshond Club of America in 1978. Her first litter, which was sired by Champion Painter of Summerville, included four champions in eight puppies. Her last litter, by Champion Fearless Flintstone, produced six champions from the nine puppies. And in between, by Champion Keenote's Sterling Silver, ROMX, there had been six champions among eight puppies.

The contribution and influence of "Cookie Monster" and "Toes" on the Keeshond breed has been tremendous, and tracing back pedigrees of numerous Kees in the show rings of today will lead in many cases to the names of one or the other of these great bitches among the forebears.

For Pound Sterling's last litter, Jean Ellis and Andrea Haberman decided again on an outcross. This time it was Champion Le Jeans Allan A Dale, C.D., "mainly because Jean felt that his dam, Champion Le Jeans Utsi, was an exceptionally lovely bitch." Champion Tryon's Gandalf the Grey and Champion Tryon's Beorn, ROMX, HOF were the two dogs shown from this litter, both glorious show dogs and beloved family pets. Gandalf has some important Group wins to his credit. Beorn has accounted for seven Group Firsts (starting at eleven months with the latest at six years) and a Specialty Best of Breed to his credit. With his son and kennel mate, Champion Cascadia Dutch Baron, he has won four Best Brace in Show awards and four others with Champion Maywood High Fashion of Modesto. Twenty-nine champions to date have been finished, sired by Beorn, among them four Group winners and two bitches that have Group placements. Carolyn Wray tells us, "Although Pound Sterling was the dam of some of the loveliest of the Tryon Kees, she is no doubt best remembered as 'Beorn's mother'. She was a very showy bitch with a beautiful head and expression, of correct size, with the short back and Keezie temperament that kept her Andrea's special pet for her lifetime."

Jean Ellis felt very strongly that Keeshonden should be family pets, and that as such they should have at least basic obedience training to make them pleasant to have around and live with. Thus obedience titles **were** a respected part of the dog's name at Tryon, and every adult dog there was obedience-trained to a novice level even if not possessing a degree.

The true obedience "star" at Tryon was Champion Fritz van Voornaam, U.D., HOF, a son of Champion Flakkee Sweepstakes, ROM, HOF, purchased by Jean and Andrea as an eleven-month old puppy. Fritz easily finished his conformation title and achieved several Group placements; but his real forte was in the obedience ring. A High in Trial Dog, several High Combined Open B and Utility scores, and many first places in the advanced classes, plus his happy attitude and attractive appearance have made him a true favorite with the public. I daresay that he has converted many a "dog fancier" to becoming a "Kees fancier."

A bitch sired by Champion Tryon's First Try also did outstanding work in the obedience rings in the Northwest: Tryon's Silver Dawn, C.D.X., trained and shown by Diana Dryden. Judy Daugherty

Ch. Fritz Van Voornaam, U.D., HOF, owned by Jean Ellis, Tryon Kennels, Oregon.

Ch. Flakkee's Choice For Tryon, C.D.X., purchased as a puppy in 1968 by Jean Ellis from the Porter Washingtons to help build the foundation for Tryon Keeshonden.

showed one of her first Kees in obedience, Cascadia Stormy Cricket, C.D., sired by Champion Tryon's Coin of the Realm. And Champion Charann Christmas Holli, C.D.X., now owned by Anna Brown, descends from Tryon dogs through both sire and dam.

A few years back circumstances necessitated that Jean Ellis discontinue breeding. Unfortunately, Andrea Haberman also found it necessary to take this step at about the same time. Carolyn Wray says, "Were it not for some dedicated Kees people, such as Judy Daugherty, Helen Wymore, Helen Cuneo, and the many others who are to be thanked for continuing on with the next generation, Tryon Kees probably would have remained only in the memory of those who had a Tryon as a loved family pet."

It is happy news for all the Kees world that Andrea Haberman is again becoming active in the breed and in November 1982 finished a beautiful bitch, Champion Cascadia Lunar Eclipse. It is hoped that she will continue to breed a small number of Tryon Kees, knowing, as she does, that great things can be achieved in the Dog Fancy without breeding so many dogs that doing justice to each becomes an impossibility.

Ch. Flakkee's Choice For Tryon, C.D.X.
(Ch. Flakkee Jackpot, ROMX, HOF X Flakkee Tango)
Whelped 5-8-68   Breeder: Flakkee Kennels

Litter # 1 Whelped 12-10-70 by Ch. Star*Kees Batman, ROMX

1) Am. and Can. Ch. Tryon's Coin of the Realm
    Ch. Frostridge Here Comes the Sun
    Ch. Frostridge Maggie Mae
     Ch. Frostridge Hazey Daisy
     Ch. Frostridge Moonlight Dancer
    Tryon's Dividend, ROM (7 points and one Major)
      Am. Can. Ch. Maladolph's Heidi-Ho of Allan
       Ch. Maladolph's Koningster
       Ch. Maladolph's Baron von Zureeg
      Ch. Maladolph's Clown Princess
      Am. and Can. Ch. Maladolph's Jo Jo
      Mbowow
      Ch. Maladolph's Starbuck
      Ch. Jo-Li's Dutch Treat of Maladolph
    Cascadia Stormy Cricket, C.D.
     Ch. Cascadia Puff O'Smoke, C.D.
    Cascadia Platinum Gypsy
     Am. and Can. Kagins Admant Beau Jest

2) Tryon's Silver Dollar
    Lauri's Nightshade, C.D.
    Tryon's Little Shadow, C.D.
     Ch. Charann Chritmas Holli, C.D.X.
     Charann Wonder Woman, C.D.

3) Am. and Can. Ch. Tryon's Pound Sterling, C.D., ROM

Litter # 1 By Ch. Flakkee Wrockhound
Ch. Tryon's Wrocky Road (Group Winner)
Ch. Tryon's Wrockin' Robin
  Ch. Charann Christmas Holli, C.D.X.
  Charann Wonder Woman, C.D.
Ch. Tryon's Wrock Festival
  Am. and Can. Ch. Ronson's Benji Boy
  Cascadia

104

Ch. Ronson's Special K, C.D.
Am., Can. and Mex. Ch. Cascadia's H R
Puff N Stuff
Can. Ch. Tryon's Little Wrock Riot
(2 Majors & Best Puppy in Specialty)
Tryon's Ms. Got Wrocks, ROM
    Am. and Can. Ch. Cascadia Menomonee
    Warrior (Group Winner)
        Ch. Mac Kees Sgt. Pepper
        Ch. Graywyn's Indian Penny
        Ch. Komagas Chip O' The Old Block
        Ch. Komagas Sitting Bull

    Ch. Cascadia Country Gentleman J
    Ch. Cascadia Captain's Pride (Group
    Winner)
    Ch. Cascadia Aslan of Narnia
        Ch. Cascadia Summer's Breeze
        Ch. Cascadia Hot Lips O'Houlihan
        Ch. Cascadia Hawkeye
        Cascadia Little Bandit, C.D.

    Ch. Cascadia Dawn Treader
        Ch. Cascadia Dutch Baron (Group
        Winner)
        Ch. Ronson's Joshua of Cascadia
        Ch. Cascadia Sugar Plum
        Ch. Cascadia Honee Jo Van Steen
        Ch. Cascadia Cartel
          Cascadia Cristalynn
            Ch. Cascadia Hot Lips O'Houlihan

Am. and Can. Ch. Tryon's Pound Sterling, C.D.

    Litter # 2 By Ch. Rich-Bob's Stormy Weather,
    ROMX
Ch. Tryon's Tuppence
    Ch. Gregory's Pittance of Tryon
        Ch. Lupini Hit Man
        Ch. Lupini Mob's Moll
        Ch. Lupini Lovely Weather

Ch. Lupini Pretty Boy Floyd
Ch. Sir Rank's Dwarrelwind Lupini
Ch. Playmate Tic-Tac of Toes
Ch. Dutch Treat Touch of Spirit
Ch. Playmate's Lullaby
Ch. Playmate Lone Ranger
Ch. Tryon's Fearless Fruehling, ROMX
Ch. Fearless Felicity
Ch. Fearless Flavor for Keeslund
Ch. Fearless Flowerchild
Ch. Fearless Flipside
Ch. Fearless Firstclass
Ch. Fearless Fortune Cookie, C.D.
(Best in Specialty)
Ch. Charmac Fortunate Happening
Ch. Charmac's Wheel of Fortune
Ch. Charmac's Fortunatelee
Ch. Fearless Fox
Ch. Fearless Fruitcake
Ch. Fearless Focal Point
Ch. Trekins Believe In Magic
Ch. Fearless Floorshow
Ch. Fearless Fanci Free of Car-Ron
Ch. Fearless Flying Tiger
Ch. Karolina Silver Star
Ch. Karolina Lone Ranger
Ch. Fearless Karolina First Lady
Ch. Fearless Fanny Fox O'Bonnyvale
Ch. Fearless Freewheeler
Ch. Fearless Framework
Ch. Fearless Firstorm
Fearless Filibuster (KCA Futurity winner)

Litter # 3 By Ch. Le-Jeans Allan-A-Dale, C.D.

Ch. Tryon's Gandalf The Grey (Group Winner)
Ch. Tryon's Beorn, ROMX, HOF (Group &
Specialty Winner)
Am. and Can. Ch. Cascadia's Menomonee
Warrior (Group Winner)

Ch. Mac Kees Sgt. Pepper
Ch. Graywyn's Indian Penny
Ch. Komagas Chip O'The Old Block
Ch. Komagas Sitting Bull
Am. and Can. Ch. Ronson's Benji Boy of Cascadia
Ch. Ronson's Special K, C.D.
Ch. Ronson's Joshua of Cascadia
Ch. Klassic's Dynamic Dame
Ch. Pogo's Deja Vu V Cascadia
Ch. Cascadia Summer's Breeze
Cascadia Little Bandit, C.D.
Ch. Cascadia Crepe Suzette
Ch. Keedox's Wendy of Cascadia
Ch. Keedox Porthos
Ch. Cascadia Puff O'Smoke, C.D.
Ch. Cascadia Honee Jo Van Steen
Ch. Maladolph's Clown Princess
Ch. Frostridge Moonlight Dancer
Ch. Cascadia Country Gentleman J
Ch. Cascadia Dutch Baron (Group Winner)
Ch. Cascadia Silmarien
Ch. Royal J. Cavalier of Kooskia (Group Winner)
Ch. Cascadia Captain's Pride (Group winner)
Ch. Cascadia Cartel
Ch. Maladolph's Starbuck
Ch. Cascadia Sugar Plum
Ch. Beorn's Triumphant TV Misty
Ch. Pogo's Percolator
Ch. Beorn's Teddy Bear V Misty
Ch. J. Beks Jackie Blue
Ch. Cascadia Aldaron
Ch. Beorn's Katrina V Misty
Ch. Jaze Wild Card of Cascadia
Ch. Cascadia H R Puff 'N Stuff
Ch. Cascadia Lunar Eclipse
Ch. Cascadia Dr. Pepper
Ch. WoffeeBrazen Detonation

Ch. Flakkee's Choice For Tryon, C.D.X.

Litter # 2 Whelped 12-12-72 by Ch. Flakkee
Instant Replay, HOF

   Ch. Tryon's Instant Love
         Ch. Conquest Foredeck Skipper
   Tryon's Instant Happiness (Major points & Best Puppy in
   Specialty)
   Tryon's Instant Fortune (Major points)
   Tryon's Instant Mischief, ROM (14 points, one Major)
         Ch. Cascadia Crepe Suzette
         Ch. J Beks Jackie Blue
         Ch. Beorn's Triumphant TV Misty
         Ch. Beorn's Katrina V Misty
         Ch. Beorn's Teddy Bear V Misty
         Tryon's Miss Kanga (Pointed)
            Ch. Pogo's Deja Vu V Cascadia
               Ch. Cascadia Summer's Breeze
               Cascadia Little Bandit, C.D.
            Ch. Keedox's Wendy of Cascadia
               Ch. Keedox Porthos
            Ch. Pogo's Percolator
            Ch. Jaze Wild Card of Cascadia
         Tryon's Edward Bear, C.D.X.

Vandy

The Vandy Keeshonden, at Ridge, New York, started in 1972 with a dog purchased from a pet shop by Carole Henry. He never saw the inside of a show ring as, to quote his owner, "he had every fault known." But he did distinguish himself in the obedience ring, becoming Vandy Thane, C.D.X., and getting his owner "hooked" on owning a show dog.

Carole researched breeders carefully the next time before making a purchase, and subsequently bought her first show Kees from Lynda Doughty in 1974. This was a ten-month-old male, as she had at that time no interest in breeding. Two years later Lynda bred her first litter making a champion from one of the bitches. So then again she was "hooked"—this time on all the various phases of raising and showing Kees.

In just eight litters, three of which were whelped during 1983, Carole had tried to breed for type, soundness and intelligence, and we must comment that she seems to have succeeded admirably in this goal!

The dog Carole purchased from Lynda Doughty grew up to become American and Canadian Champion Dow-Tee's Easy Rider, C.D.X., Canadian C.D. Born June 20th 1973, sired by Champion Dalbaco Beachcomber, ROMX, from Champion Von Storm's Katy Did, C.D., ROM. He was Carole's first show dog, and he was owner-handled and trained by her. His conformation wins include Best in Show at the prestigious Westbury Kennel Association event in 1977 under judge Jerome Rich; 54 Bests of Breed, five Bests of Opposite Sex, nine Group placements, and twice Group 1 here in the United States. While in Canada, where he was shown six times, he was twice Best of Breed (winning the Group on one of these occasions, and placing third on the other) and five times Best of Winners.

In the obedience ring, "Boo" won five High in Trial awards; was invited to represent the Keeshond breed in the Gaines Obedience Drill Team at Westminster 1979 and is the first Best in Show winning Keeshond to have gained an advanced obedience degree.

Additionally, this magnificent dog is the first Keeshond to have won the top awards in BOTH conformation and obedience offered by the Keeshond Club of America. In 1975 he was Top Obedience Dog, KCA; in 1977 Top Show Dog.

Additionally, "Boo"is making his presence felt as a sire, with both champions and obedience titlists to his credit.

Champion Vandy's Argo, C.D., born on October 13th 1976, was bred by Carole Henry, by Champion Dow-Tee's Easy Rider, C.D.X. from Dow-Tee's Little Darling. This bitch finished from the Bred-by Exhibitor Class with two 4-point "majors" in eight shows, defeated only once in the breed classes.

In obedience she was shown five times, earning three firsts, and tied twice for first place. In 1979 she won the Dog World Award and had the highest national average for Keeshonden that year, 1975.

Argo's first breeding was to Champion Candray Ghost of Winter Green. Four puppies from this litter were shown, becoming Champion Vandy's Bayonne, C.D.X. (dog), Champion Vandy's Breagan, C.D. (Best of Breed winning bitch, also a High in Trial winner); Vandy's Bayou, C.D. (who is "major" pointed), and Vandy's Beta, C.D. (also "major" pointed).

Ch. Vandy's Argo, C.D. (right) by Ch. Dow-Tee's Easy Rider, C.D.X. from Dow-Tee's Little Darling here is completing her title with a four-point "major" by going Best of Winners at Bucks County 1978 from the classes. Her sire (on the left) was Best of Breed. These excellent Kees are owned by Carole Henry, Ridge, New York.

For her second breeding Argo went to Champion Candray's the Nobleman, which produced Champion Vandy's De Ja, and for her third and last litter the chosen sire was Champion Fearless First Class. These puppies were born in October 1983 and three are in show homes.

Memorable dog shows for Carole Henry have included the Heritage Trail Keeshond Specialty on April 30th 1983, where Argo's daughter, Champion Vandy's Breagan, C.D. took High in Trial with 198½; and another Argo daughter, Champion Vandy's De Ja won the large Open Bitch Class. In addition, her granddaughter, Vandy's Chanti, took first in Bred-by and Reserve Winners Bitch.

Then on June 4th and 5th in 1983, at Huntington Valley and Delaware County Kennel Clubs, under judges Dr. Samuel Draper and Mrs. Tom Stevenson respectively, Argo's son from her first litter, Vandy's Bayonne, C.D.X., and Argo's daughter from her second litter, swept both shows taking two 4-point "majors"—both finishing on the second day.

Argo, now retired from the whelping box, finds life very agreeable as a "bed" dog, a pleasure she has well earned!

The homebred bitch, Champion Vandy's Breagan, C.D., was the "runt" of the litter, but she was born a show girl. From the time she made her debut at the match shows, when she never took less than Best Puppy in Match (six matches, four Bests in Match, twice Best Puppy), right through gaining her championship, from Bred-by Exhibitor with four Bests of Breed and four Bests of Opposite Sex, all with competition, and on in to "specials" where she was shown eight times, winning three Bests of Breed with male "specials" competing and twice Best of Opposite Sex, she made her presence felt every inch of the way.

In obedience all of her scores were over 195, with a High in Trial (198½), and her average was 196.5 to finish her C.D.

Breagan's first breeding was back to her grandsire. One of these puppies has been shown, and needs three points to finish. The second time around Champion Tanglewood Mark Frost was the stud chosen for her. Two of these offspring have been shown, one of which has already gained a "minor"; and as they are just a year old as we write, there are more to come!

Windrift

Joanne Sanford Reed, owner of Windrift Keeshonden at Canyon Country, California, had enjoyed the companionship of several different breeds while she was growing up, having been the type of child in whom animals seemed to immediately recognize a friend, truly a "natural" with them.

German Shepherds were her breed, training in obedience, when for the first time she set eyes on a Keeshond. He was the top obedience dog in her class, and Joanne could not get over his beauty and his intelligence. Another German Shepherd handler, Sandy Kreuger, shared Joanne's admiration for this Kees, and so the two of them set out to find a Keeshond bitch whom they could show and breed.

The result of some careful searching was Joanne's first Keeshond, Traveler's Zeedrift Carioca, daughter of Champion Zeedrift Kwikzilver, HOF, ex Zeedrift Booty, purchased from breeders Ralph and Charlene Sims. Born on January 22nd 1968, "Cari" lived to be a bit over twelve years old, and the contributions she made to the Keeshond breed were inestimable in their greatness.

Sandy Kreuger and Joanne Reed took turns showing their beautiful new Kees puppy, and had put more than half her points on before her puppy coat started to drop, and so it was decided to stop showing and to breed her before trying to complete her championship. Her show career was only interrupted, as after producing puppies she came back to gain her title, and as a producing dam she also earned a place in the Registry of Merit.

Selecting exactly the right stud for "Cari" was given much thought and study, with the eventual selection of the great winner Champion Flakkee Jackpot, HOF, ROMX. As Joanne comments, "for her first litter, she did seem to start with a silver spoon in her mouth," as two of these puppies grew up to become champion Flakkee Instant Replay, HOF, and Champion Windrift's Midnite Masquerade.

The breeding to Jackpot was repeated—not once but twice, and "Cari" added Champion Flakkee High Roller (numerous Group placements) and Champion Windrift's Blackjack (a Group First winner) to her progeny.

Then in 1974 "Cari" was bred to Champion Star-Kees Batman, ROMX, in which litter she produced Champion Windrift's Batwoman and Canadian Champion Windrift's Robin.

And so Windrift was on its way, its very first litter from its foundation bitch having accomplished what breeders sometimes dream about for years without ever really hitting it!

Soon Joanne was making a goodly number of new champions to add to the Windrift roster. During this period she was working as an assistant handler for Ric Chashoudian when one day the two of them "discovered" Star-Kee's Dingbat at a show they were attending, and were delighted to learn that his owner, Robin Stark, was interested in selling him. Needless to say, Dingbat was immediately purchased. He went on to become a three times Best in Show winner, the Best of Breed at two National Specialties, and the love of Joanne's life. To date (January 1984) "Dinger" has produced 27 champions, making his ROMX. Also he has earned a position in the Hall of Fame.

Champion Windrift's Midnite Love, HOF, came after Dingbat, and became the Top Specialty Winner of all time, winning, in 1976, Nor Cal Keeshond Club, Heart of America Keeshond Club, the Keeshond Club of America National, and Evergreen Keeshond Club. In 1977 he led the Keeshond Club of Southern California and the Sahuare State Keeshond Club. And in 1978 he was winner of the Keeshond Club of Southern California Specialty. Additionally, he had many Group wins

Ch. Star-Kee's Dingbat, C.D., HOF, ROMX, pictured just after winning his first all-breed Best in Show at Contra Costa Kennel Club, June 1974.

The foundation bitch at Windrift Kennels, Ch. Traveler's Zeedrift Carioca, ROM, by Ch. Zeedrift Kwickzilver, HOF ex Zeedrift Booty. Bred by Ralph and Charleen Sims.

A gorgeous front view of Ch. Windrift's Willy Weaver, sire of the Best in Show winning Ch. Windrift's Gambler, C.D. ROM, by Ch. Star-Kees Dingbat, HOF, ROMX ex Windrift's Wonder Woman. Bred by Joanne Reed and Pam Hardie.

Ch. Windrift's Midnite Special, bred by owner Joanne Reed, is the sire of Ch. Windrift's Midnite Love, who was the # 1 Kees for 1976 and is the all-time Specialty winner.

and placements. Midnite Love was sired by Champion Windrift's Midnite Special from Windrift's Love of Cari.

Midnite Love got Joanne's parents, George and Dorothy Jacobson, to whom she gave him for part of his career involved in showing Kees. This dog has more Specialties to his credit than any other Kees alive, and Joanne believes that her dogs have won more Specialties in total than those of any other Kees kennel.

Champion Windrift's Lover Boy was next in line. Another successful Group dog, "Romeo" won three Group Firsts and numerous placements before being sold to his present owner, Les Baker of New York for whom he is doing well on the East Coast.

Then for a change of pace, Joanne retired temporarily (at least partially) from "specialing" a *dog* and helped Kris Arnds campaign with a *bitch*, Champion Windrift's Love Unlimited, who was by Champion Rich-Bob's Stormy Weather, ROMX from Windrift's Lovelace, ROM. This lovely bitch also became a Group winner and twice a Specialty Best of Breed winner, which definitely is not easy in this breed. She is still going strong.

Champion Windrift's Gambler, C.D., HOF, was America's # 1 Kees in 1982. Shown during 1982 and 1983 he has, as of December 1983, two all-breed Bests in Show, twelve Group Firsts, and 36 additional Group placements. Also he has won three Independent Specialties, including the 1982 National. He finished his requirements for the Hall of Fame at two and a half years old, and gained his C.D. title in three consecutive shows. Gambler is by Champion Windrift's Willy Weaver ex Champion Windrift's Hollywood Squares, was bred by Joanne Reed, and is owned by John and Tawn Sinclair.

Gambler, known to his friends as "The Dog," it is felt, has an unusually successful career ahead of him as a sire, as in the first year his offspring have been shown, six of them already have become champions.

Willy Weaver, in addition to being Gambler's sire, is also the sire of Champion Chalice's Silver Horizon (from Champion Windrift's Silver Chalice) who is well to the top of the Keeshond winners for 1983, having created somewhat of a sensation in the East under Doug Holloway's handling. Horizon is owned and was bred by Cindy Nary.

American and Canadian Champion Windrift's Oscar for A.B.C., by Dingbat ex Academy Award, is owned by Jack and Arlene Grimes who co-bred him with Joanne Reed. Born June 10th, 1981, he gained his American championship at exactly thirteen months of age, having taken a Best of Breed and a Best of Opposite Sex along the way. At two and a half years old, he now has added five more Bests of Breed and two Group Firsts to his record. In Canada, at his only Specialty, he won Best Puppy in Sweepstakes, finished his title at two years and two months old, and has added three Bests of Breed and two Group placements since then.

Academy Award, Oscar's dam, also is owned by Jack and Arlene Grimes and Joanne Reed, being by Champion Windrift's Midnite Love, HOF, ROM, ex Windrift's Wonder Woman, ROM. She is the dam of three American Champions (Oscar, American and Canadian Champion Windrift's producer, and American and Canadian Champion Windrift's Show Stopper, the first two by Dingbat, the third by Gambler). She completed her American championship at two years of age, and during 1982, in 49 shows entered and 13,520 miles travelled, owner-handled all the way, she gained eight Bests of Breed, two Group Fourths, and 27 Bests of Opposite Sex, including the Northern California Specialty. In Canada she has been undefeated so far in all twelve shows entered for Best of Opposite Sex, including a Canadian Specialty. Academy Award is # 2 Keeshond Club of America Top Kees Bitch for 1982, # 3 bitch and # 10 Kees that same year on the *Keezette* (magazine) scoreboard.

As we write this book, Joanne Reed is grooming her new young dog for 1984 and '85. He is Champion Windrift's Producer, by Champion Star-Kee's Dingbat ex Champion Windrift's Academy Award, bred by Jack and Arlene Grimes and Joanne Reed. This is Joanne's last son of the great Dingbat (who is well, happy, and enjoying life as of January 1984, but is no longer siring). He is already off to a flying start, having won the Keeshond Club of Southern California Sweepstakes in 1982 and the Dallas Keeshond Club Sweepstakes in 1982.

Joanne Reed has had a very diversified background in the world of pure-bred dogs, which obviously equipped her well to succeed with her own kennel. Moving into Los Angeles a few years back, she worked in a Standard Poodle kennel part time, training their champions in obedience. From that experience she acquired two Standard Poodles which she showed in conformation, and she is the breeder of

Opposite page:
Ch. Windrift's Love Unlimited, HOF, by Ch. Rich-Bob's Stormy Weather, ROMX ex Windrift's Lovelace, ROM. Bred by Joanne Reed, owned by Kris Arnds. This Keeshond has won 88 times Best of Opposite Sex, twice Best in Specialty, and four times Opposite Sex in Specialty.

one Poodle litter. During her moves around Southern California, at one point she lived close to Ric Chashoudian's kennel, where she was in the habit of boarding and grooming her dogs. Then she became Ric's assistant, making shows with him, and became his bookkeeper. She comments, "I have had the benefit of his experience in various ways, including training, showing, conditioning, grooming and breeding. I had shown many a famous winning Terrier to first in Group, and also had the privilege of raising Champion Joni's Red Baron of Crofton, the top Lakeland Terrier of all time. I won the first Group placement with this dog, and being responsible for him was a great honor."

Mrs. Reed has owned and bred Airedales, and also Labrador Retrievers. Her son, Kevin Reed, just thirteen years old, is very much involved with Joanne's Kees, helping to raise and care for them. Three years ago he wanted a Rottweiler for his own. It took a year to find him the lovely bitch Windrift's Atari Von Printz, who finished her championship for them at twelve months of age, "mostly from the 9-12 puppy class going Best of Opposite Sex over 'specials'." At this time the Reeds are planning to breed Rotties as well as the Kees. Joanne's great hope is that her son may one day decide to handle dogs for others.

Joanne and her husband, George Reed, have a small Arabian horse operation, and have thoroughly enjoyed success showing and breeding them. Joanne closes with the remark that "I must give my husband credit. Were it not for his patient understanding, I would never have been able to achieve what I have with the Kees."

As of December 1983, Joanne Reed has bred or owned more than 52 Kees champions.

Best in Show winners, either owned, bred, or from the Windrift line, include:

Ch. Flakkee Instant Replay, HOF
Ch. Star-Kee's Dingbat, C.D., HOF,
  ROMX
Can. Champion Windrift's Hot Shot
Can. Champion Windrift's Dr.
  Bombay
Ch. Windrift's Gambler, C.D.,
  ROM
Ch. Chalice Silver Horizon,
  HOF

Group First winners:
Just Windrift
  Ch. Windrift's Midnite Love, HOF
  Ch. Windrift's Blackjack
  Ch. Windrift's Love Unlimited, HOF
  Ch. Windrift's Lover Boy
  Ch. Windrift's Sundance
  Ch. Windrift's Fair N' Square
  Ch. Windrift's Willy Weaver
  Ch. Windrift's Oscar for A.B.C.

Specialty Best of Breed winners:
Just dogs bred or owned
  Ch. Star-Kee's Dingbat, C.D.,
    HOF, ROMX
  Ch. Windrift's Midnite Love, HOF
  Ch. Windrift's Love Unlimited,
    HOF
  Ch. Windrift's Lover Boy
  Ch. Windrift's Gambler, C.D.,
    HOF, ROM
  Ch. Windrift's Willy Weaver

**Champions bred or owned
by Windrift:**
  Ch. Traveler's Zeedrift Carioca,
    ROM
  Ch. Windrift's Midnite Masquerade
  Ch. Flakkee Instant Replay, HOF
  Ch. Windrift's Midnite Special
  Ch. Star-Kee's Dingbat, C.D.,
    ROMX, HOF
  Ch. Windrift's Dynamic Duo
  Ch. Windrift's Midnite Love, HOF
  Ch. Flakkee High Roller
  Ch. Windrift's Single Edition
  Ch. Windrift's Batwoman
  Ch. Windrift's Sunday Love
  Ch. Windrift's Butterfly
  Ch. Windrift's Assassinator
  Ch. Windrift's Buckwheat
  Ch. Windrift's Hot Shot
  Ch. Windrift's Robin
  Ch. Windrift's Instigator
  Ch. Windrift's Blackjack

Ch. Windrift's Midnite Express
Ch. Windrift's Cover Girl
Ch. Windrift's Love Unlimited
Ch. Windrift's Lover Boy
Ch. Windrift's Dr. Bombay
Ch. Windrift's Fortune Teller
Ch. Windrift's Captain Midnite
Ch. Windrift's Sundance
Ch. Windrift's Hollywood Squares
Ch. Windrift's Fair N'Square
Ch. Windrift's Fearless Fascinate
Ch. Windrift's Honey Bear
Ch. Windrift's Willy Weaver
Ch. Windrift's Lovelee Ureka
Ch. Windrift's Call Girl
Ch. Windrift's Gambler, HOF
Ch. Windrift's Circuit Breaker
Ch. Windrift's Annie Oakley
Ch. Windrift's Winkist
Ch. Windrift's Peter Pan
Ch. Windrift's Academy Award
Ch. Windrift's Silver Chalice
Ch. Windrift's Music Man
Ch. Windrift's Honky Tonk
Ch. Windrift's Oscar of A.B.C.
Ch. Windrift's Producer
Ch. Windrift's Stormy Love
Ch. Windrift's Mercy Sakes
Ch. Windrift's High Society
Ch. Windrift's Bloomer Girl
Ch. Windrift's Sharp Shooter
Ch. Windrift's Drummer Boy
Ch. Windrift's Marksman
Ch. Windrift's Show Stopper

A youthful picture of Ch. Keeboom's Sir Thomas owned by Brian and Yvonne Gray, vonRyan Kennels, Saskatchewan Canada.

120

Chapter 5

Keeshonden in Canada

It was a lovely bitch from England, Alex of Evenlode, imported by Miss M.E. Butler of Montreal, from the famed Evenlode Kennels of Miss Hastings, who established a pair of "firsts" for the Keeshond breed in Canada. She it was who introduced the breed to the Canadian Fancy, arriving there in March of 1929 and registered the following October. She also was the first to exhibit at the Canine Society of Montreal in June 1930, under a judge from the United States, Mr. Tom Hissey. Alex was a daughter of Den Helder from Grania.

Miss Butler was obviously the first important Canadian Kees fan. Another of her dogs, David of Evenlode, became the first of the breed to earn a Canadian Championship, and we find records of him being entered at Ladies Kennel Club of Canada in both 1931 and 1933, and at the Montreal Kennel Association as well during the latter year. Bred by Mrs. Master, David was a son of Cely von Jura de Witt ex Lufton Liefje. Another bitch belonging to Miss Butler, Netherlands Breda, was also shown in the early 1930s.

Miss Hilda White, of Toronto, made an appearance in 1933 at the York Kennel Club Dog Show held in Aurora, Ontario. She created quite a stir with seven Keeshonden, all either owned or bred by herself. Among her importations were Hansel van Zaandam, by Alli von der Sternwarte from Champion Gesina van Zaandam, who was bred by Mrs. Wingfield Digby. And Gipsy van Leyden, by Guelder Geron ex Suntje van Zaandam, bred by Miss Wallace. These two were imported in 1930 and 1931 respectively. Dirck van Zaandam of Fairlands and Hals van Zaandam, both youngsters from these two, were exported to the United States. Miss White evidently called hers the "van Zaandam" kennel, although this famous kennel identification was officially registered in England exclusive to Mrs. Wingfield Digby.

Mrs. Alice Toole of West Calgary, Alberta, was another early enthusiast for the breed, and in 1937 registered six of them; they included the imported dog, Orange Jorie, a grandson of Guelder Alewin bred by Mr. J. Galloway.

From this beginning, Kees have been steadily admired by Canadian fanciers, and in these modern times there are a number of kennels of them flourishing there. They include Betty Olafson's Rokerig Keeshonden at Palgrave, Ontario, who owned the famous American and Canadian Champion Racassius of Rhinevale, ROMX, an important dog in Kees history, born in 1968.

Klompen Kennels, owned by Kathy and Bruce Stewart, are at Sydney, Nova Scotia. Famous winners here include Canadian Champion Klompsen's Limejuice Lill, by Wistonia Winter Wind ex Canadian and American Champion von Ryan's Ragamuffin, Canadian C.D., who is a Canadian Group and Best in Show bitch. Canadian Champion Klompen's Sluicebox Sam (a brother to the above) was a Best in Show dog. And numerous other dogs of quality and merit.

The Paladin Kees are at Locust Hill, Ontario, where they are owned by the Jack Nugents. Headman here would be the handsome thirteen-year-old Canadian and American Champion Paladin's Jolly Roger, while we have also heard words of praise for the excellent Canadian and American Champion Paladin's Deputy Dawg, Canadian Champion Paladin's Shooting Star, Canadian Champion Paladin's Bashful Bentley, and other glorious Kees carrying the "Paladin" identification.

Maureen Clements, at Geluk Kennels, Salisbury, New Brunswick, owns a glorious dog in Canadian and American Champion and Canadian and American Obedience Trial Champion Geluk Is Prince Igor—a dog of fabulous quality who has made history in the show ring and in obedience competition. His record speaks for itself. Another marvelous dog from here is American and Canadian Champion Geluk Is King Liam's Fancy, C.D.X., who is by American and Canadian Champion Racassius of Rhinevale ex American and Canadian Champion and Obedience Trial Champion Geluk Is Tarantella. It is interesting to me, as a great admirer of the Japar dogs, that Tarantella is a granddaughter of Champion Japar Fearless Knight, one of the finest from this excellent mid-West U.S.A. kennel.

Seawind Keeshonden are at Tantallon, Nova Scotia. Don and Gladys Gates are owners of Canadian Champion Kristlkees Kelaina of Seawind, Canadian C.D., who is a Group placing Best of Breed bitch in the conformation ring, a multiple High in Trial Obedience winner, and the dam of champions, including Canadian Champion Seawind's Lit'l Bit O'Wrock and Canadian Champion Seawind's September Schatzie.

There are various other prominent and successful kennels in Canada breeding Kees, one of the finest of which is vonRyan Kennels, whose story follows.

The vonRyan Keeshonden, at Gray, Saskatchewan, Canada, are owned by Brian and Yvonne Gray who purchased their first Kees in 1973 as a pet, Canadian Champion Chan-Star's Silver Baron, C.D.X., who was a son of Champion Sir Anton Rodrigo Montgomery ex Marganna's Silver Beauty. Obviously Silver Baron more than fulfilled his owner's expectations, as, although bought as a pet, he became a multiple Group placing dog, an exuberant worker in obedience, and was a member of Canada's first national Scent Hurdle Champions, the "Blazing Saddles," a title he and his team-mates held for four consecutive years.

The Grays purchased Champion Keeboom's Sir Thomas (Champion Flakkee's Keeboom Import ex Champion Brialin's Josedale Witt's Pride) from Dr. Peter Witt, Toronto, in 1975, who became a Group placing dog.

Then came the foundation brood bitch, Champion Baronwood's Hot Dam (Champion Flakkee Jackpot ex Champion Picvale's Miss Vixen of Banks), purchased from Donna and Gene Smith in Florissant, Missouri, in 1976. Hot Dam did very well in the show ring, becoming Top Kees Bitch in Canada in 1977, a multiple Group placer, and Best of Opposite Sex at the Keeshond Breeders and Fanciers Association of British Columbia Specialty in 1977.

It was as a producer, however, that Hot Dam really came into her own. She was bred in 1978 for the first litter to Champion Flakkee Instamatic, one of Porter and Dickie Washington's great dogs, and the resulting litter included Champion vonRyan's Oop C. Daisy (finished as a puppy with numerous Puppy in Group and two Puppy in Show wins, one in Bermuda); American and Canadian Champion vonRyan's Jiffy James (multi-group placing dog, # 3 Kees in Canada 1981, # 2 Kees in Canada 1982); American and Canadian Champion vonRyan's Ragamuffin (owned by Bruce and Kathy Stewart of Sidney, Nova Scotia, and a Best in Show dog with numerous Puppy in Group and in Show wins when younger); and American and Canadian Champion Flakkee vonRyan's Express, owned by the Porter Washingtons.

Can. Ch. Baronwood's Hot Dam, by Ch. Flakkee Jackpot ex Ch. Picvale's Miss Vixen of Banks, foundation brood bitch at vonRyan Kennels, Brian and Yvonne Gray, Saskatchewan. She is a multi-group placing bitch and was Top Kees Bitch in Canada in 1977. Bred by Donna and Gene Smith, Baronwood's Kennel, Florissant, Missouri, purchased by the Grays in 1976.

Ch. vonRyan's Dam Good Lookin' is the most promising of the young show dogs at vonRyan's Kennels, Saskatchewan, Canada.

Ch. vonRyan's Oop C. Daisy, by Ch. Flakkee Instamatic from Ch. Baron-wood's Hot Dam. Brian and Yvonne Gray, breeders-owners, vonRyan Keeshonden, Saskatchewan, Canada.

In 1980 Hot Dam was again bred to a Flakkee dog, in this case the choice having been Champion Flakkee Instant Replay. From this litter came Champion vonRyan's Grand Slam, shown to his championship but never "specialed" as the Grays were campaigning Jiffy James.

For their next litter, in 1981, the Grays bred the bitch Champion vonRyan's Oop C. Daisy to their Champion vonRyan's Grand Slam. Champion vonRyan's Sharp Shooter was in this litter, along with the well named Champion vonRyan's Dam Good Lookin'. The latter bitch finished Top Bitch in 1982; Top Puppy Kees in 1982, and Number 6 (Male/Female) in 1982. The Grays consider this one to be their most promising show prospect to date and, although they will be breeding her in 1984, they want to keep her in competition right up until the very last moment. She was Best of Opposite Sex in 1983 at the Keeshond Breeders Association of British Columbia Specialty in Langley, B.C.

The Grays have kept their breeding program geared to the Flakkee line, feeling that these dogs best exemplify what they want to see in a Kees insofar as those very important considerations, such as size, soundness, temperament and expression, are concerned.

125

Aust. Ch. Gurawin Domenique, by Delft Blauw Vaandrig ex Aust. Ch. Karuah Black Velvet, bred by Mrs. M. Langdon, is the foundation bitch belonging to Peter and Lynda Churchward at North Richmond, New South Wales, Australia. This lovely Kees produced three champions in her very first litter.

Chapter 6

The Keeshond in Australia

We are very much impressed with the truly excellent Keeshonden being produced in Australia, and proud at having a most representative group of breeders and dogs of which to tell you here. A study of the accompanying illustrations will back up the reasons for my admiration of these dogs; and many words of praise for the Kees "down under" have reached my ears through the comments of leading United States judges who have officiated there recently.

Looking back into history, we find that Mrs. G. Bourne, living in New South Wales, is generally credited with having introduced the Keeshond to Australia, more than thirty years ago, with the importation of four handsome members of the breed which came over to her from England. These dogs were representative of Britain's leading bloodlines of the day, and were Champion Valies of Vorden, C.D.; Champion Airking of Arnhem; Airamber of Arnem; and Babette of Willoden.

It was in 1956 that Mrs. Hannaford is credited with having bred a litter of Kees, on which we find no further details beyond the fact that Mrs. Hannaford was using the kennel-name Wistonia, but that her dogs were in no way related to England's famed Wistonia Kennel which played so major a role in the development of the Keeshond in Great Britain and in the United States. As we find no later references to Mrs. Hannaford's dog, we assume this to have been a somewhat passing activity for her.

During this same year Bob Lucas had started what was to become a successful kennel and a long time interest in Kees which is still active as we write in 1983. "Marybob" was originally his kennel prefix, later changed to "Lucullus." He met with considerable success during the 1960s with a Kees named Derbydale Dixie, who amassed a notable collection of "in show" and Group victories.

Derbydale Kennels themselves brought at least several good dogs from Western Australia to New South Wales, eventually locating in Western Australia.

Another Kees enthusiast of the early 1960s, Beryl Parry who was located at Peterborough, was extremely active in both conformation and obedience competition. Three or more champions are credited to her; two of hers gained C.D. titles in obedience, and the Top Novice Dog in Australia were all included, we understand, in one litter of nine bred by this lady.

Classification for Kees at a Royal Show was provided for the first time in 1962, with only one being entered. The peak entry at a Royal for the breed during those years was in 1966 when twelve of them were listed.

Over the years, breeding and show stock has been imported to Australia, particularly to the New South Wales area and to Western Australia. Among the champions who have come in have been Waakzaam Weismuller, Duroya Janessa of Dargrant, Ledwell Jasper, Ledwell Intrepid, Waakzaam Walsoken, Waakzaam Wolthuis and Gavimar Ubacaan, Ensign of Duroya, Duroya Charming Angel, Valsgate Broth of a Boy, Lekdon Zabadak of Duroya, Duroya Homeguard, and Vanglede Hypernion.

Among the very enthusiastic and dedicated Keeshond breeders now active in Australia are Peter and Lynda Churchward, who started out with Kees in 1976. The Churchwards' foundation bitch, Australian Champion Gurawin Domenique, was born in September 1976, a daughter of Delft Blauw Vaandrig and Australian Champion Karuah Black Velvet, bred by Mrs. Langdon. She was the first of six Keeshonden to have attained Australian championships by the close of 1983 for the Churchwards, and is highly valued for her lovely temperament as well as for her correctness of type. Nikke distinguished herself by producing three Australian Champions in her first litter, of which the sire was Australian Champion Makoro Sir Benjamin.

The lovely Benjamin was the first of the Churchwards' Keeshond males, a son of Australian Champion Colijn Toby Tyler and Australian Champion Aak Babette who was born in February 1977, bred by Ida and Ernie Evans. A consistent winner in his younger days, Benjamin has two Best in Show awards to his credit, along with two

Windrift Hollywood Squares is exhibiting what dog shows are all about as she displays the joy of winning after taking a 5-point Specialty win her first time out in the Bred-by Exhibitor Class. Owned by Joanne Reed, Windrift Keeshonden, Canyon Country, California.

Aust. Ch. Makoro Genevieve, a very keen competitor in the ring, owned by Peter and Lynda Churchward, North Richmond, New South Wales.

Best in Group awards and numerous age classes "in Group" and "in Show." A highlight of his career was being awarded Best in Show at the Non-Sporting and Working Dog Club in the State of South Australia when important wins for the breed were rare. In order to make way for the younger dogs, Benjamin is shown sparingly now but has become a prominent winner in the Veteran's Sweepstakes.

Homebred Australian Champion Tiburon Alexander, by Australian Champion Makora Sir Benjamin ex Australian Champion Gurawin Domenique, was born in June 1980. He is one of the three champions

Aust. Ch. Colijn Van Kerel, the noted Australian Best in Show winner, owned by Peter and Lynda Churchward.

from the first litter of the two aforementioned original Churchward-owned Kees. He is the winner of Best in Show All-breeds, and also was Best Dog at the April 1982 New South Wales Keeshond Club Specialty Championship Show, as well as many age classes in Group and in Show.

By far the most successful to date of the Churchwards' dogs has been Australian Champion Colijn Van Kerel, by Australian Champion Colijn Pal Joey from Australian Champion Colijn Karelle, born in September 1979 and bred by Mrs. Beryl Douglas who is a widely esteemed breeder, long active in the Australian Kees Fancy. Pal Joey, from everything we have heard about him, is a true credit both to the Colijn strain and to the Churchwards. In the eighteen months to December 1983 he has won seven all-breed Bests in Show, fifteen Bests in Group, three times has been Runner Up to Best in Show, numerous age classes and "in Group" and "in Show," while remaining a steady winner in Best of Breed competition.

The Churchwards' second bitch, Australian Champion Makoro Genevieve, daughter of Australian Champion Gavimar Ubacaan (import from the U.K.) and Australian Champion Colijn Gaykee was born in October 1978, bred by Ida and Ernie Douglas. Her sire, Ubacaan, has been a highly successful addition from England to Mrs. Beryl Douglas' kennel, and this bitch has been a keen and notable con-

Aust. Ch. Keesbury Lady Carina, by Aust. Ch. Colijn Silver Kapitan ex homebred Aust. Ch. Tiburon Anastasia, at three months of age. Born July 1982, bred by David and Judith Berry. This young bitch is a consistent winner at breed level for her owners, Peter and Lynda Churchward, North Richmond, New South Wales, Australia.

Aust. Ch. Ryfrost Silver Knight is a consistent Challenge Certificate and Reserve Certificate winner at most Royal Shows of the early 1980s in Australia. Owned by Mr. and Mrs. E. Ryan, Ryfrost Kennels, Young, New South Wales.

Ch. Keeboom's Sir Thomas, by Ch. Flakkee's Keeboom Import ex Ch. Brialin's Josedale Witt's Pride, purchased from Dr. Peter Witt, Toronto, Ontario, in 1975 by Brian and Yvonne Gray, as an early member of their vonRyan Kennels, at Saskatchewan, Canada.

Aust. Ch. Rymiska Little Gem, Best Puppy in Show at the 1983 Sydney Royal is a daughter of Aust. Ch. Ryfrost Pan Jack. Owned by Mr. and Mrs. E. Ryan, New South Wales, Australia.

Aust. Ch. Ryfrost Capten Stalite, born July 2nd 1982, is a son of Aust. Ch. Rymiska Kzam ex Ryfrost Silver Lady. He is owned by Mr. and Mrs. E. Ryan, Young, New South Wales.

tender in the show ring. Throughout her career she has been consistently a winner of the Best Bitch award and it is not uncommon for her, even now at five years age, to gain the Best of Breed award.

Latest addition to the Churchwards' kennels is the Australian Champion Keesbury Lady Carina, by Australian Champion Colijn Silver Kapitan from Australian Champion Tiburon Anastasia. Bred by David and Judith Berry, her dam is the litter sister to Alexander, and she is starting now to make her mark in the Kees world, being, at the age of only one year, already a regular winner at breed level. Also as a line-bred bitch she is felt to be the future of the Tiburon strain.

Mr. and Mrs. E.J. Ryan, owners of Ryfrost Kennels at Young in New South Wales, have been breeding Keeshonden since the beginning of the 1970s. Champion Ryfrost Pan Jack was in one of the first litters the Ryans bred, and they have continued along the same bloodlines until the late 1970s when they brought in an English import who has blended very well with their original breeding program. This was the handsome Champion Duroya Homeguard.

The Ryans have now teamed up with friends of theirs in Sydney, Ray and Marilyn Parker, owners of the Rymiska Kennels, who had some of their stock at the time. For the past few years these two kennels have been breeding together, and the Ryans are very pleased with the fact that their dogs have been gaining Challenge Certificates at the Royal Shows in Brisbane, Sydney, Melbourne, and Adelaide.

Australian Champion Ryfrost Captain Stalite, a young dog born in 1982, took Best of Breed at the Winter Classic in Sydney judged by Richard Beauchamp from the United States; Best in Show at the Keeshond Club of Victoria, judged by Mrs. A.M. McDonald from the United Kingdom, and was runner-up to Best of Breed at the Spring Fair.

Ryfrost Robyn's Pride won a Challenge Certificate at six months of age at the Winter Classic in Sydney under Mr. Beauchamp, the Bitch Challenge at Brisbane Royal 1983, Best Puppy of the Day at Melbourne Royal in 1983, Minor in Show at Keeshond Club of Victoria, and was Challenge bitch at the Spring Fair in Sydney 1983.

Australian Champion Rymiska Little Gem, who is a daughter of Australian Champion Ryfrost Pan Jack, won Best Puppy in Show at the Sydney Royal in 1983 and has already had an exciting career by the end of that year, while Australian Champion Rymiska Kzam, sire of Ryfrost Robyn's Pride and Champion Ryfrost Capten Stalite, is distinguishing himself in both the show ring and as a stud dog. This

135

Ch. vonRyan's Grand Slam making a good Puppy Group win under judge Ed Dixon. Owned by Brian and Yvonne Gray, vonRyan Kennels, Saskatchewan, Canada.

Am. and Can. Ch. Pied Piper of Fairville shows off his correct expression and good reach of neck as he wins the breed at Wilmington in 1981. Joan Toombs, owner, Wilmington, Delaware.

Barb Bagwell, Hanna City, Illinois, with Hi Struttin' Banner Girl, C.D.X., eight and a half years old when this picture was made, going High in Trial at Scott County Kennel Club, May 1982. By Nordeen's Qasion ex Nordeen's Victory Girl, bred by Velvabell Nordeen.

son of the Ryans' imported Champion Duroya Homeguard during the early 1980s has gained an impressive number of Challenge Certificates at the Royal shows.

Another widely admired Challenge winner at the Royals has been Australian Champion Ryfrost Silver Knight.

The Ryans are thoroughly dedicated fanciers who truly enjoy their dogs and have many plans for the future of their kennel.

Ray and Marilyn Parker, owners of the Rymiskas with whom the Ryans have been working so successfully, purchased their first show Kees from Mrs. Beryl Douglas at the time of their marriage. Long before then Mr. Parker had seen and loved the breed, but misfortune with his earliest purchases had temporarily cooled his enthusiasm.

Ryfrost Pan Jack was the Parkers' first show dog, having been purchased with the understanding that he would be exhibited. Mrs. Parker learned about grooming through this dog, and as her confidence increased she showed him herself, doing a bit of winning. Next came Colijn van Johdie who attained his Australian Championship, followed, in 1979, by the Parkers' first bitch, Colijn Miska, bred and purchased from Mrs. Douglas. After an inauspicious beginning Miska's ring career started gaining speed, in the form of Best in Show wins at two successive Keeshond Specialties.

Soon after that the Parkers purchased a dog puppy, Ryfrost Silver Knight, from the Eddie Ryans of Ryfrost Kennels. What fun and excitement this dog has provided for them! At twelve months of age he won Best in Group and Best Junior in Show at an important all-breed show under distinguished judge L.L. De Groen; in 1982 he was awarded the Challenge Certificate at the Sydney Royal Easter Show, and his successes have continued steadily ever since.

Meanwhile, home at the kennel, Champion Colijn Miska was bred to the Ryans' import, Champion Duroya Homeguard, producing Rymiska Kristy Lee and Rymiska Kzam, a bitch and a dog respectively, both of whom were kept by the Parkers. Kzam has been a source of deep pride to the Parkers and to the Ryans, with such wins as Reserve Challenge Certificate in 1982 while still a puppy at the Sydney Royal, repeating it later that year at the Adelaide Royal. Then at Australia's largest show, the Melbourne Royal, he won the dog Challenge Certificate in keenest competition.

For her second litter, born May 1982, Miska was bred to Ryfrost Pan Jack. Six puppies again, one bitch this time retained by the Parkers. By nine months of age this puppy had become a champion,

Aust. Ch. Rymiska Kzam, a son of Ch. Duroya Homeguard, is the sire of Ryfrost Roby's Pride and of Ch. Ryfrost Capten Stalite. Photo courtesy of the Ryans, Ryfrost Kennels.

Aust. Ch. Ryfrost Pan Jack was bred by the Ryans in one of their very first litters, and is behind many of the currently successful Ryfrost dogs. Mr. and Mrs. E. Ryan, Young, New South Wales, Australia.

The famous Ch. Holland Hond's Landmark winning a Group First under Miss Virginia Sivori. Landmark is a Hall of Fame and a Register of Merit dog. He has 75 Bests of Breed, 34 Group placements, and six Group Firsts to his credit. Owned by Carol J. Aubut, Tanglewood Kennels, Westford, Massachusetts.

Miss Judith Gurin with Ch. Holland Hond's Landmark. Following his retirement from conformation he went on to Junior Showmanship with his friend, Judy, and won many first prizes. Carol Aubut, owner, Westford, Massachusetts.

Winning the Non-Sporting Group at the prestigious Tuxedo Kennel Club Dog Show, under Australian judge Peter Thomson, is Cynthia Nary's outstanding dog, Ch. Chalice's Silver Horizon, with his handler Douglas R. Holloway. A top winner of 1983.

had gained two Best in Group awards, and in April 1983 was Best Exhibit in Show at the New South Wales Keeshond Club Specialty in an entry of 86. On Easter Monday she gained Best Puppy in Show at the Sydney Royal.

Miska has been bred again, shortly before we are working on this book, this time to the recent English import, Hanovarian Silver Moonlight. Considering her record as a producer, something very worthwhile undoubtedly will result this time, too.

Keeshee Kennels own some very fine Keeshonden, belonging to C. and M. Sheehy at Riverwood in New South Wales. Their young dog (born in 1981), Australian Champion Keeshee Pug Mahorne, has been enjoying an exciting career, and from March 1982 up to December 4th 1983 had accounted for all-breed Bests in Show at Manly and District and Newcastle Merewether Combined Canine Club, both during October 1983, along with twice Runner Up to Best in Show, twenty Classes in Show, nine Best in Group, 30 Classes in Group, and numerous exciting Sweepstakes wins, among them the 1983 Spring Fair Open Sweepstakes.

This dog was bred by R. and V. Clancy but is owned by the Sheehys, from their homebred bitch Australian Champion Keeshee Balka.

Both parents of Pug Mahorne have succeeded well in the show ring. Zacht, who was born in April 1980, has been twice Runner Up to Best in Show, has won many Classes in Show, plus a goodly number of Best in Group and Classes in Group. He is by Australian Champion Delft Blauw Hollander (Champion Waakzaam Wolthuis, imported from the United Kingdom, ex Delft Blauw Saffer) ex Australian Champion Delft Blauw Anjelier (Australian and New Zealand Champion Waakzam Walsoken, imported from the United Kingdom, ex Colijn Azuur).

Balka, also, has won Classes in Show and Classes in Group. Born in October 1978, she is a daughter of Australian Champion Parlevink Jerrold (Kuruah Kimberly—Colijn Danee) ex Australian Champion Colijn Silver Penny (Australian Champion Ledwell Jasper, imported from the United Kingdom, from Australian Champion Colijn Miss Vixen). In addition to being the dam of Pug Mahorne, this splendid bitch has produced the very exciting puppy, Keeshee Shantelle, with a Best Baby Puppy in Show at three months old, who was sired by R. and M. Cleverly's well-known dog, Australian Champion Delft Blauw Maestro, strongly bred to the Waakzam line.

Headstudy of Aust. Ch. Keeshee Pug Mahorne, handsome young homebred who has made an exciting show record for breeders-owners C. and M. Sheehy, Keeshee Keeshonden, Riverwood, New South Wales.

Aust. Ch. Keeshee Balka is the winner of many Classes in Show and many Classes in Group. Owned by Keeshee Keeshonden, C. and M. Sheehy, Riverwood, New South Wales.

Left: *(Above)* "Amy," seven years old and now retired at home, is better known to her public as Ch. GreenKees Kismmet V Ledwell, by Eng. Ch. Ledwell Kardos ex Pure Honey of Ledwell. Owned by Mr. and Mrs. William Eckhart, GreenKees Kennels, Greenland, New Hampshire.

Opposite page: *(Above)* Tanglewood Kennels presents a new champion for 1983. Ch. Tanglewood Ivanhoe, by Ch. Holland Hond's Landmark ex Tanglewood Darcy, owned and handled by Carol J. Aubut.

First place in the Brood Bitch Class at the 1980 Keeshond Club of America National Specialty won by Sonja Sobaka of Holloridge, ROM. Her offspring pictured: Am. and Can. Ch. Sobaka's Steppenralf, Am. and Can. C.D.; Am. and Can. Ch. Call Me Leon T. Sobaka, Am. and Can. C.D.; Am. and Can. Ch. Sobaka Rodean Ado Annie, Am. and Can. C.D.; and Am. and Can. Ch. Sobaka Charlie's Angel. Sonja was the foundation bitch at Sobaka Kennels, owned by Patricia Katomski-Beck, Plattsmouth, Nebraska.

145

Ch. Tanglewood Magic Marker of Kavancha, Pam Fedder's U.S.A. import for her Kavancha Kennels in Welkom, South Africa, who has done some exciting winning and proven a superb stud dog in his new home. Purchased from Carol Aubut in the United States.

Chapter 7

Keeshonden in South Africa

There is a very well-known Keeshond Kennel in South Africa, Kavancha, owned by Pam Fedder, located at Welkom. It was in 1979 that Pam and Chris Fedder came to the United States where they attended the Keeshond Club of America National Specialty. The purpose of their trip was to locate and import a bitch who would bring new blood to their country as foundation stock for their kennel.

At the Specialty, the Fedders saw and particularly admired Champion Holland Hond's Landmark, Carol Aubut's noted dog and decided then and there that they would like one of his daughters. Carol was duly contacted and yes, she did have one Mark daughter which she had been planning to keep for herself. Also she had a male puppy from a Mark daughter and sired by Mark which obviously was very strong in this line. The Fedders made an appointment to come to see both, and after much discussion with full appreciation that the dog puppy did have the advantage of being DOUBLY Mark-bred, they decided that they would like to have him.

So it was that on Friday, July 27th 1979, Tanglewood Magic Marker of Kavancha left Logan Airport in Boston en route to Frankfurt, Germany, scheduled to arrive in Johannesburg, South Africa, on Sunday morning.

Marker, we are told, made the trip with ease, settled into his new home as though he had always lived there, and soon embarked on what has now become a most impressive show career.

By the time he had reached eighteen months of age, "Markie" had won twelve Challenge Certificates, twelve Bests of Breed, eight Group placements, a Best in Show, and four Bests in Show at "afternoon

Ch. Tanglewood Magic Marker, son of Ch. Holland Hond's Landmark, was exported by Carol S. Aubut to South Africa where he has become a Best in Show winner.

Opposite page: *(Above)* Ch. Rhinevale Ribstonpippin, by Eng. Ch. Ledwell Dutchman ex Eng. Ch. Raffetta of Rhinevale, was bred by Margo Emerson, Rhinevale Keeshonden, Claygate, Surrey, England. This was the 1975 Top Winning Member Owned Dog from the Heritage Trail Keeshond Club, and is owned by Mr. and Mrs. William Eckhart, GreenKees Kennels, Greenland, New Hampshire. *(Below)* Ch. Ledwell Britannia, by Eng. and Am. Ch. Keesland Fisherman ex Ledwell Quetta, finished in eight weeks, never out of the ribbons and taking three "majors" en route to the title. Bred by Mrs. Sylvia Scroggs, Oxon, England, Handled by L. Mae Evans. Owned by Mr. and Mrs. William Eckhart, GreenKees Kennels, Greenland, New Hampshire.

shows" which we understand are events similar to our own match show events. His wins have been made under such famed international judges as Dr. Spiro from Australia, United States experts Jacky Hungerford and Jim Bennett, Mrs. van Ommen Kloeke from Holland, Major Harry Glover and Barbara Jupp from England, and Mrs. Furst Danielson from Sweden, among others.

Mark's first show was a Championship Show in October following his arrival. He was entered in Minor Puppy Class, which he won; then competed in Open Class where he placed third, something unusual, to say the least, for a Kees puppy!

Although the first from America, there are other fine imported Kees in South Africa as well, mostly from the United Kingdom; plus some good homebreds. The Fedders, prior to Mark, owned Champion Rhinevale Rochmador of Chattaronga who, very sad to report, died of a severe nose-bleed en route to a "double" dog show weekend in Rhodesia, a 1,100-mile trip from their home. They travelled with four other people, including the driver and a total of eight dogs going to be shown (in addition to the Fedders and their Kees, there were three Pyrenean Mountain Dogs, a Pyrenean Sheepdog, a Tibetan Spaniel, and the Fedders' two Keeshonden), by bus, as roads had been made unsafe by terrorist attacks; the bus, in fact, was to have an armed escort convoy. Needless to say, the death of their one dog took all the fun out of it for the Fedders, especially since the veterinary care they were able to find for him was hardly adequate. But having travelled that far, they did go on with the show, and when it was all over they had won the Dog Challenge Certificate with their other Kees, Kavancha Bounty Hunter, not once but at BOTH of the dog shows, where the judging must have been very consistent as Champion Bach of Ven was also Best of Breed both days and Champion Ledwell Dorinda was Best of Opposite Sex. Probably this was the Fedders' most memorable dog show trip, due to the danger involved and its various traumas. But I guess dog show folks are the same throughout the world in determination and willingness to go through hardships to get us to the show!

The first Keeshond to be registered in South Africa belonged to a fancier in Cape Town, but there is evidently no record of whether or not it was ever shown.

The first pair was imported by the late Mr. Michael Lupton in 1951, their names Trusty van Saandam and Heena of Summerlease. Interest in the breed increased, and in 1959 Casper van Saandam was the first Keeshond to win a Best in Show, this at Bloemfontein. Several Kees since then have Best in Show honors to their credit; one of the most impressive records, Pam Fedder tells us, was that of Champion Waakzaam Wroom of Chattaronga, who went Best in Show on three occasions including Goldfields Kennel Club, the largest dog show held in South Africa.

The Michael Luptons were breeders of enormous importance in the South African Keeshond world. Originally they used the kennel prefix "van Saandam" but later changed it to "Sedbergh," which became noted for some especially lovely dogs. Michael and Vera Lupton imported many Kees from England and from Ireland. One of the latter, Champion Geronina of Brytondale, carried the white gene and threw an occasional white pup amongst her grays.

Later Mrs. Eva Ficker started in Kees, importing two Dutch champions from Holland Sigelinski's Siem and Sigelinski's Marjan for her van Saaftingen Kennels, which were very famous. Siem won Best in Show at Goldfields in 1961. He was one of the leading stud dogs of his time. Mrs. Ficker has also passed away, so "van Saaftingen dogs" are no longer being bred.

The Keeshond Club was founded in 1962. Michael Lupton served as Chairman until 1969, then was succeeded by Dave de Kock until 1972 and since then Percy Green has been Chairman. The Club's first Championship Show took place in 1968.

Other Keeshonden important to the progress of the breed in South Africa have included a lovely Best in Show dog owned by Mrs. van Wyngaardt; then another one, Champion Drostdy's Wilmington Herman, owned by Mr. and Mrs. Jim Simmons, Americans who had been living in S.A. temporarily, who took Herman with them when they returned to the United States.

Carol Ruzow imported a handsome male from England, Champion Waakzaam Wroom of Chattaronga, the aforementioned three-time Best in Show winner. A beautiful bitch bred by Carol out of Wroom, Champion Chattaronga Camille, has been the Top Winning Bitch in South Africa for quite some time now, and was Best in Show at the Keeshonden Club Championship event recently. Ian Stubbings in East London's Champion Vandersee Addition went Best in Show at both an All-Breed event and a Utility Show (which is about on a par with our Non-Sporting Group) and then his other dog, Champion Vandersee Ad Lib, also went Best in Show at a Utility Show.

Can. Ch. and O.T.Ch. Tigger's Moonshadow, Can. and Am. U.D. doing a Utility bar jump, the "wahoo" expression on his face showing his obvious pleasure. Owned by Ellen and Tom Crewe, Moonshadow Kees, Green Bay, Wisconsin. Photo by Ellen.

152

Ch. Chan-Star's Silver Baron, C.D.X., by Ch. Sir Anton Rodrigo Montgomery ex Marganna's Silver Beauty, first Kees purchased as a pet by Brian and Yvonne Gray in 1973. He distinguished himself as a multi-Group-placing dog, in obedience, and in his work as part of the "Blazing Stallions," Canada's first national Scent Hurdle Racing Champions for four consecutive years.

Ch. Vandersee Ad Lib, a lovely example of the Keeshond quality to be found in South Africa. Mr. and Mrs. I. Stubbings, owners. Picture courtesy of Pam Fedder.

This is the famed Ch. Waakzaam Wroom of Chattaronga, felt by many to be the leading Kees in South Africa's dog show competition to date, with his three all-breed Bests in Show. Imported from England by Carol Ruzow, now owned by Pam Fedder.

South African Ch. Rhinevale Rochmador of Chattaronga, famous winning Keeshond owned by Mrs. Pam Fedder, Welkom, South Africa.

We understand that Carol Ruzow contributed greatly to the Keeshond as a breed in South Africa, importing dogs from both the Rhinevale and the Waakzaam Kennels in England. One dog she imported from Rhinevale, later purchased by Pam Fedder, became Pam's own Champion Rhinevale Rochmador. When Carol gave up Kees in favor of Poodles, Pam purchased her excellent stock, and Rocamador was one of her favorites whom she made a champion and who won a lot of Group placements. Also, the famous Champion Waakzaam Wroom of Chattaronga became Pam's, together with the others.

Adding to the story of Pam bringing her beloved "Markie" to South Africa, Pam bred her homebred bitch, Champion Kavancha's Anneline, to this U.S. importation from Carol Aubut's stock, keeping a male from the litter, Kavancha's Gotcha. In five shows this youngster has gained four Challenge Certificates, one Reserve, and four Bests of Breed. Also, he won the Group under Edd Bivin when the latter judged there recently. Since a South African Championship is gained by winning five points earning Challenge Certificates, the latter amounting to either one or two points each, depending on the number of entries, (the judge reserving the right to withhold a C.C. for lack of

Misazar's Attention Seeker, Am. C.D.X., Can. C.D., #2 in Obedience, *Keezette* System, for 1982 and probably 1983, by Ch. Grawyn's Hot Shot ex Jake's Mistake of Misazar, Am. and Can. C.D.X. Bred by Dr. R. Stephen Willding and Joy Ann Willding and owned by Joy-Ann Willding, Schaumberg, Illinois.

Opposite page: Am. and Can. Ch. Dow-Tees Easy Rider, C.D.X. and Can. C.D. by Ch. **Dalbaro** Beachcomber, ROMX, from Ch. Von Storms Katydid, C.D., ROM, was bred by Lynda Doughty and is owned by Carole Henry, Ridge, New York. "Boo" was Ms. Henry's first show dog, owner-handled and trained. Shown here winning the Veteran Dog Class at the Delaware Valley Specialty in 1979 at the age of seven years.

South African Ch. Vandersee Addition owned by Mr. and Mrs. I. Stubbings, East London, South Africa. Photo courtesy of Pam Fedder.

merit) and Gotcha is so close to it, we are sure he will have his title when you read this.

Pam Fedder inserts this note of interest, "Many years ago, I mated two greys, of course both carrying the white gene, and produced two whites and one grey puppy. One of the whites went to Holland to become International Champion Kavancha's Now or Never. A picture is enclosed of two of his offspring mated to a white bitch. He has only been used at stud on white bitches in Holland, and has only produced whites. I later exported a grey to Holland, Kavancha's Blyth Spirit, who also became a Dutch Champion. I have to date been the only kennel in South Africa to export Keeshonden back to Holland."

In 1980, Ian and Elaine Stubbings came to South Africa from England with their two English Champions, Final Edition of Duroya and Duroya Josephine of Vandersee, who was the Top Winning Keeshond in the United Kingdom at that time. They have produced two lovely Best in Show dogs in South Africa, and will certainly leave their mark on the breed in that country.

There are a few recent newcomers to the Fancy in South Africa, but they have still to prove themselves by breeding champions. At this point it seems quite obvious that Kavancha and Vandersee Kees are the two top breeding kennels for Kees in South Africa at the present time.

158

Chapter 8

Standards of the Keeshond

What is the Standard of the Breed?

The Standard of the Breed, to which one hears such frequent reference whenever purebred dogs are the subject of discussion, is the word picture of the ideal specimen of a breed of dog. This standard outlines, in specific detail, each and every feature of that breed, both in physical characteristics and in temperament, accurately describing the dog from whisker to tail, creating a clear impression of what is to be considered correct or incorrect, the features comprising "breed type," and the probable temperament and pattern of typical members of that breed.

The standard is the guide for breeders endeavoring to produce quality dogs, and for fanciers wishing to learn what is considered beautiful in them. It is the tool with which judges evaluate and make their decisions in the ring. The dog it describes is the one which we seek and to which we compare in making our evaluations. It is the result of endless hours spent in dedicated work by knowledgeable members of each breed's parent Specialty Club, resulting from the combined efforts of the club itself, its individual members, and finally the American Kennel Club by whom official approval must be granted prior to each standard's acceptance, or that of any amendments or changes in it in the United States. Breed standards are based on intensive study of breed history, earlier standards in the United States or in the countries where the dogs originated or were recognized prior to introduction to the United States, and the purposes for which the breed was originally created and developed. All such factors have played their parts in the drawing up of our present standards.

159

Ch. ABC's Zaffree Gypsy, C.D. (left) and Ch. ABC's Gypsy Zev (right) winning Best Brace at the Keeshond Club of America Specialty. Owned by Jack and Arlene Grimes, Martinez, California.

Ronson's Thomas' Tamara To Love, C.D., T.D.X. owned by Patricia A. Thomas, Lansing, Michigan.

This picture of Eng., Am., and Can. Ch. Wrocky of Wistonia was selected by the Keeshond Club of America as the ideal Standard of the Breed. Shown 36 times in the U.S.A. and Canada, this remarkable dog was Best of Breed 35 times, Best Non-Sporting Dog 33 times, and Best in Show eighteen times. Mr. and Mrs. Porter Washington, owners, Flakkee Kennels, Lawndale, California.

Official American Standard for the Keeshond

GENERAL APPEARANCE AND CONFORMATION: The Keeshond is a handsome dog, of well-balanced, short coupled body, attracting attention not only by his alert carriage and intelligent expression, but also by his luxurious coat, his richly plumed tail well curled over his back, and by his foxlike face and head with small pointed ears. His coat is very thick round the neck, fore part of the shoulders and chest, forming a lionlike mane. His rump and hind legs, down to his hocks, are also thickly coated forming the characteristic "trousers." His head, ears and lower legs are covered with thick short hair.

The ideal height of fully matured dogs (over 2 years old), measured from top of withers to the ground, is: for males, 18 inches; bitches, 17 inches. However, size consideration should not outweigh that of type. When dogs are judged equal in type, the dog nearest the ideal height is to be preferred. Length of back from withers to rump should equal height as measured above.

HEAD: **Expression**—Expression is largely dependent on the distinctive characteristic called "spectacles"—a delicate penciled line slanting slightly upward from the outer corner of each eye to the lower corner of the ear, coupled with distinct markings and shadings forming short but expressive eyebrows. Markings (or shadings) on face and head must present a pleasing appearance, imparting to the dog an alert and intelligent expression. *Fault:* Absence of "spectacles."

Skull—The head should be well proportioned to the body, wedge-shaped when viewed from above. Not only in the muzzle, but the whole head should give this impression when the ears are drawn back by covering the nape of the neck and the ears with one hand. Head in profile should exhibit definite stop. *Fault:* Apple head or absence of stop.

Muzzle—The muzzle should be dark in color and of medium length, neither coarse nor snipy, and well proportioned to the skull.

Mouth—The mouth should be neither overshot nor undershot. Lips should be black and closely meeting, not thick, coarse, or sagging; and with no wrinkles at the corner of the mouth. *Faults:* Overshot or undershot.

Teeth—The teeth should be white, sound and strong (but discoloration from distemper not to penalize severely); upper teeth should just overlap the lower teeth.

Eyes—Eyes should be dark brown in color, of medium size, rather oblique in shape and not set too wide apart. *Fault:* Protruding round eyes or eyes light in color.

Ears—Ears should be small, triangular in shape, mounted high on head and carried erect; dark in color, and covered with thick, velvety short hair. Size should be proportionate to the head—length approximating the distance from outer corner of the eye to the nearest edge of the ear. *Fault:* Ears not carried erect when at attention.

BODY: **Neck and Shoulders**—The neck should be moderately long, well shaped and well set on shoulders; covered with a profuse mane, sweeping from under the jaw and covering the whole of the front part of the shoulders and chest, as well as the top part of the shoulders.

163

Ch. Flakkee Instamatic winning the Non-Sporting Group at Pocatello, Idaho, judged by Anna K. Nicholas. Porter Washington handling for Flakkee Kennels, Lawndale, California.

Ch. Ruttkay Sirius, HOF, by Can. and Am. Ch. Sinterklaas Brave Nimrod ex Ruttkay Smoky's Heidi Ho. Sirius is the top winning son of one of the breed's great producers. His credits include 158 times Best of Breed, 15 times Best Non-Sporting Dog, 75 Group placements, two all-breed Bests in Show and two Bests of Breed at Keeshond Specialty Shows. Bred by Ruttkay Kennels, owned by Elizabeth C. Ginsberg.

Am. and Can. Ch. Pied Piper of Fairville going Best of Breed at almost five years of age. The Fairview dogs mature slowly and hold their beauty over a good length of time. In November 1983, at six years, he was shown four times, taking Best of Breed on three of these occasions, gaining two additional Group placements at the same time. Jean C. Toombs, owner, Wilmington, Delaware.

Chest, Back and Loin—The body should be compact with a short, straight back sloping slightly downward toward the hindquarters; well ribbed, barrel well rounded, belly moderately tucked up, deep and strong of chest.

Legs—Forelegs should be straight seen from any angle. Hind legs should be profusely feathered down to the hocks—not below, with hocks only slightly bent. Legs must be of good bone and cream in color. *Fault:* Black markings below the knee, penciling excepted.

Feet—The feet should be compact, well rounded, catlike, and cream in color. Toes are nicely arched with black nails. *Fault:* White foot or feet.

TAIL: The tail should be set on high, moderately long, and well feathered, tightly curled over back. It should lie flat and close to the body with a very light gray plume on top where curled, but the tip of the tail should be black. The tail should form a part of the "silhouette" of the dog's body, rather than give the appearance of an appendage. *Fault:* Tail not lying close to the back.

ACTION: Dogs should show boldly and keep tails curled over the back. They should move cleanly and briskly; and the movement should be straight and sharp (not lope like a German Shepherd). *Fault:* Tail not carried over back when moving.

COAT: The body should be abundantly covered with long, straight, harsh hair; standing out well from a thick, downy undercoat. The hair on the legs should be smooth and short, except for a feathering on the front legs and "trousers," as previously described, on the hind legs. The hair on the tail should be profuse, forming a rich plume. Head, including muzzle, skull and ears, should be covered with smooth, soft, short hair—velvety in texture on the ears. Coat must not part down the back. *Faults:* Silky, wavy or curly coats. Part in coat down the back.

COLOR AND MARKINGS: A mixture of gray and black. The undercoat should be very pale gray or cream (not tawny). The hair of the outer coat is black tipped, the length of the black tips producing the characteristic shading of color. The color may vary from light to dark, but any pronounced deviation from the gray color is not permissible. The plume of the tail should be very light gray when curled on back, and the tip of the tail should be black. Legs and feet should be cream. Ears should be very dark—almost black. Shoulder line markings (light gray) should be well defined. The color of the ruff and "trousers" is generally lighter than that of the body. "Spectacles" and shadings, as previously described, are characteristic of the breed and

166

must be present to some degree. There should be no pronounced white markings.

Very Serious Faults: Entirely black or white or any other solid color; any pronounced deviation from the gray color.

Scale of Points

General conformation and appearance		20
Head	6	
Eyes	5	
Ears	5	
Teeth	4	
Body		35
Chest, back and loin	10	
Tail	10	
Neck and shoulders	8	
Legs	4	
Feet	3	
Coat		15
Color and markings		10
Total		100

Approved July 12th 1949

Interpretation of the Standard

Learning the words of a breed standard is not all that difficult. Many people can recite them verbatim, with great confidence and few mistakes. The important thing, however, is that this not be a parrot-type procedure, or a case of knowing the words but not understanding what it is that they are saying. The exercise of mechanically repeating what is written in a standard is of insignificant value UNLESS accompanied by a true understanding of these words to the point where one becomes able to apply them to the dogs themselves. This is the area where people sometimes fall short, occasionally even including judges.

Once a Keeshond fancier has thoroughly acquainted himself or herself with the standard's words, then it becomes important to cultivate the habit, every time one looks at a member of the breed, of mentally comparing this dog to those words. Some dogs will adhere closely to them; others will not. The Keeshond fancier, especially one planning to become a breeder, or an exhibitor, or perhaps one day a judge, should never miss the opportunity of learning to apply

Ch. Geronimo's Katie O'Trup at Pontiac Kennel Club, August 1983. Mary Alice Smiley owns the Geronimos at Midland, Michigan.

Prize Package of Fairville, by Ch. Maverick Son of Ilka ex Ch. Nimble Nina of Fairville, finished her title in November 1982. Marguerite K. Goebel, owner, Chadds Ford, Pennsylvania.

As an eight-month-old puppy, Fairville's Round Trip went Best of Breed from the classes at Lackawanna in 1983. Jean C. Toombs owner, Wilmington, Delaware.

Ch. Rockhold Frolic of Ramsgate is one of the splendid winning Kees owned by Zoe W. Bemis and Charlotte White.

familiarity with the standard's specifications to each feature of every Keeshond seen. You'll be amazed at how quickly and how well you can thus teach yourself to look knowledgeably upon the dogs, and to mentally evaluate the degree of quality each possesses.

From the moment we started discussing purebred dogs, we have learned that *type* is the magic word for the basic requisite of a show quality member of *any* breed. But do we truly *understand* the word, and of what correct type consists??? What about balance, without which no animal can be truly excellent, even though possessing an outstanding individual feature, or several? Then there is soundness, to which people usually refer when speaking of the manner in which the dog gaits.

Type is a composite of the features, as outlined in the standard of each breed, which keep that breed unique and create an individuality setting it apart from all other breeds of dog, making it instantly recognizable as being what it is—a Keeshond, or a Poodle, or whatever. In the case of the Keeshond, this uniqueness is achieved by a combination of his correctly balanced head with its alert, "foxy" and intelligent expression, enhanced by the typical penciling of eyebrows and spectacles which are of tremendous importance. His medium size, sturdiness, and compactness of body; his well-feathered tightly curled tail, highset and carried flat on the back help to create the typical silhouette, as does his profuse, correctly colored and well-fitted coat of which we will speak more further along. His action is self-confident, clean, smooth and brisk. He does NOT move in a stilted manner behind, as his hocks are *slightly* bent—more so than, for example, in the Chow—but also not *overly* angulated.

The correct size of a fully grown Kees should be eighteen inches at the withers for dogs, seventeen inches for bitches. Oversized Kees are not desirable, and if the difference in overall quality is only slight, the dog of correct size is to be preferred. That dog is of better type.

Balance is a matter of proportion, and of tremendous importance as without it a dog somehow fails to look *right*, no matter how splendid the single features may be. Well balanced Keeshonden present a pleasing picture of symmetry, every part and every feature fitting into one another in such a manner as to make the dog an eye-catching example of correctness and beauty. Balance starts with the head, which should be of medium size in relation to the total dog, its muzzle of medium length, neither too pointed nor too heavy, in relation to the skull, and the ears proportionately small.

The neck is an important part of balance, and we have upon occasion noted many that were too short, detracting from the total picture. Correctly, the neck should approximate about one quarter of the dog's total length from skull to rump for correct carriage of the head.

It should be noted that although the Keeshond is to be COMPACT in build, a *square* dog is not mentioned in the standard and the one does not necessarily mean the other. Modern breeders have done well in correcting the tendency towards the excessive body length judges noticed a few years back, and one observes with pleasure that the winning dogs do appear compact, as should be the case. A low-slung Kees is not a *typical* or *well balanced* Kees. We are glad to see this being replaced by the compact and stylish silhouette created by a short back, proper length of neck, head that balances and well carried tail curled flat to the back. To complete the picture of balance, the Keeshond should look sturdy (but not coarse), with moderate bone, good depth and breadth of chest, brisket coming to the elbow.

The Keeshond coat figures in both type and balance, as, combined with ideal color and markings, it is a component of type and helps create balance. Mere quantity of coat is not enough. In fact if overdone it can create a lack of balance. The coat must be of correct *quality* and *texture*, and should be at its best when a dog is shown. Soft coats, parting down the back, are entirely atypical. Stubby broken looking coats have no place in the show ring. You will find more on this important subject covered by Carol Aubut a bit further along. There is considerable variation in the shading of Kees coats, ranging from very dark to much lighter. This is governed by the amount of black tipping on the guard hairs (outer coat) and so long as the color is definitely *gray*, both are correct. Please note that black, or smuttiness, on the lower part of legs or on the feet is objectionable. Also the facial penciling and markings should give a pleasant, attractive expression.

We have already referred to the manner in which a Keeshond should gait—as in this breed this comprises a distinctive part of "type." The hindlegs being of only *slight* angulation it is impossible for the dog to move with more than moderate drive as hind legs of this type cannot reach far under the dog. They are, however, not the almost straight rears of the Chow Chow; thus, too stilted action is not correct, but a happy medium somewhere between that of a Chow and that of a breed more angulated (than the Keeshond). Kees should move along briskly, in a straight, clean, sharp manner, carrying themselves proudly, head up and tail over the back. No judge should tolerate Keeshonden being

This handsome Kees is Ch. Foxfair's Persuasive Friend, by Am. and Can. Ch. Racassius of Rhinevale, ROMX, from Ch. Vaaker's Mary Poppins, ROM. Bred by Debbie Dorony, this magnificent Kees, an all-breed Best in Show dog and a Keeshond Club of America Best of Breed, is proudly owned by Gloria Marie Marcelli, Golden, Colorado.

Can. Ch. and Obed. Trial Ch. Tigger's Moonshadow, Can. and Am. U.D. at close to eight years old. Owned by Moonshadow Kees, Tom and Ellen Crewe, Green Bay, Wisconsin.

raced around the ring. Such action is utterly atypical of the breed and *never* should be encouraged. This writer, as a judge, dislikes intensely the current fad of racing all dogs madly around the ring, regardless of their breed or type. We are not trying to judge how fast a dog can move when we ask to see one gaited. Our purpose is to study whether or not the movement is in accordance with *correctness for the breed*. The faster the dog is travelling, the more difficult it becomes to tell how well (which is a grand way of veiling atypical movement); the correct speed is MODERATE, allowing the dog to go naturally, all four feet on the ground.

There are no breed disqualifications in the Keeshond Standard. Those imposed by the American Kennel Club, however, for dogs of all breeds are, of course, effective. These tell us that a dog who is blind, deaf, castrated, or spayed; a dog who has been changed in appearance by artificial means (except as specified in its individual breed standard); or a male who does not have two normal testicles normally located in the scrotum, may not compete at any A.K.C. dog show. The exception to this is that a castrated male may be entered in the Stud Dog Class; or a spayed bitch in Brood Bitch Class since in these cases only the progeny is judged, not the sire or dam.

A dog who is lame, whether temporarily or permanently, may not be judged and should not be brought into the ring. Such dogs must be dismissed from competition by the judge, who notes the fact and reason alongside that dog's entry number in the Judges Book. Dogs bearing a disqualification are likewise dismissed from the ring, with the notation "disqualified" in the Judge's Book accompanied by the reason.

British Standard

GENERAL APPEARANCE: A short, compact body; alert carriage, foxlike head; small pointed ears; a well-feathered, curling tail, carried over the back; hair very thick on the neck, forming a large ruff; head, ears and legs covered with short thick hair. Dogs should move cleanly and briskly (not lope like an Alsatian) but movement should be straight and sharp. Dogs should show boldly.

Head and Skull: Head well proportioned to the body, wedge-shaped when seen from above; from the side showing definite stop. Muzzle should be of medium length, neither coarse nor snipy.

Eyes: Dark with well-defined spectacles.

Ears: Small and well set on head, not wide and yet not meeting.

Mouth: Should be neither over nor undershot, upper teeth should just overlap under teeth and should be white, sound and strong (but discoloration from distemper not to penalize severely).

Forequarters: Forelegs feathered, straight, with good bone and cream in colour.

Hindquarters: Hind legs should be straight, showing very little hock and not feathered below the hock. Cream in colour.

Feet: Round and cat-like with black nails.

Tail: Tightly curled, a double curl at the end is desirable. Plume to be white on the top where curled, with black tip.

Coat: Dense, and harsh (off-standing), dense ruff and well feathered, profuse trousers; a soft, thick, light-coloured undercoat. Coat should not be silky, wavy or woolly, nor should it form a parting on the back.

Colour: Should be wolf, ash-grey; not all black or all white, and markings should be definite.

Weight and Size: The ideal height is 45.7 cm (18") for dogs and 43.2 cm (17") for bitches, but type is of more importance.

Faults: Light eyes, prominent eyes. Curly or wavy tendency in coat. Silky coat. Absence of spectacles. Nervous demeanour. Drop ears. Whole white foot or feet. Black marks below the knee, pencilling excepted. White chest. Apple head or absence of stop.

Note: Male animals should have two apparently normal testicles fully descended into the scrotum.

Australian Standard

Except for the precise conversion of English units to metric units with respect to the heights of dogs and bitches, the Australian and English Standards are identical.

176

Ch. Chan-Star's Silver Baron, C.D.X., with his team mates, Canada's first national Scent Hurdle Racing Champions, "The Blazing Saddles," a title he and his team mates held for four consecutive years. Silver Baron was the first Kees owned by vonRyanKennels, having been purchased by Brian and Yvonne Gray in 1973 as a pet.

This beautiful and typical puppy grew up to become Ch. Ruttkay The Heiress, by Ch. Ruttkay Heir Apparent ex Ruttkay Replica of Muundawg.

178

Chapter 9

The Purchase of Your Keeshond

Careful consideration should be given to what breed of dog you wish to own prior to your purchase of one. If several breeds are attractive to you, and you are undecided which you prefer, learn all you can about the characteristics of each before making your decision. As you do so, you are thus preparing yourself to make an intelligent choice; and this is very important when buying a dog who will be, with reasonable luck, a member of your household for at least a dozen years or more. Obviously since you are reading this book, you have decided on the breed—so now all that remains is to make a good choice.

The Keeshond as a Family Dog

If you are interested in a dog as a household companion who will grace your home with intelligence and beauty, make an ideal companion and canine friend for you and your children, add warmth and beauty to your life, and serve as a reliable guardian of your house and property, it would be just about impossible to improve upon a Keeshond. These delightful dogs are super-intelligent, extremely handsome, sturdy, while at the same time "handy home size," versatile, and adaptable. They delight in human companionship, being very definitely "people dogs." They demand very little in the way of special coddling and care, and will amaze you by their capabilities for learning and for getting on well with man or beast.

The Keeshond is not a quarrelsome dog; therefore is not prone to problems with other pets, whether they be members of your own household or neighboring ones. They love children, playing happily

A typical Kees puppy from Mary Alice Smiley's Geronimo Kennels at Midland, Michigan.

Ch. Windrift's Academy Award with her several-day-old litter by Ch. Windrift's Gambler, C.D., in February 1983. Jack and Arlene Grimes, owners, Martinez, California.

At four and a half months old, future Ch. Lupini Pretty Boy Floyd stands smartly at attention. Joan Magliozzi, owner, Lupini Kennels.

Ch. Sobaka Addie Its A Papermoon, C.D., by Am. and Can. Ch. Sobaka Schultz ex Am. and Can. Ch. Sobaka Rodean Ado Annie, Am. and Can. C.D. Bred by P. Katomski-Beck and A. Adler. Owned by Elizabeth Bradford and Patricia Katomski-Beck. Pictured in 1981 when just eight weeks old. A C.D. at 16 months and now a champion, too.

Am. and Can. Ch. GreenKees Beowulf v Ledwell at about eight weeks. An excellent example of a future show Kees. Owned by Mr. and Mrs. Wm. Eckhart, GreenKees Kennels, Greenland, New Hampshire.

(and gently) with them by the hour. They delight in human companionship, much preferring family living to being in a kennel. Instinctively friendly, they are quick to get on with people; but at the same time are properly suspicious of strangers until they have noted your approval.

The superiority of Keeshond intelligence, ease of learning, and anxiousness to please is affirmed by the hundreds of them who have distinguished themselves at the highest levels in obedience over the years. There would seem to be no more easily trainable a dog, as they are quick and eager to learn. For that reason you are doing yourself and the dog an injustice when you fail to provide at least the basic obedience schooling which will make him a source of even greater pleasure to live with. As show dogs they are also one of the most manageable and easiest breeds. Being a natural breed, they require no elaborate grooming but keep in good shape with a daily brushing and occasional bath, which makes them ideal for those who prefer the "do it yourself" challenge rather than a breed which must be turned over to a professional in order to be properly presented or competitive in the ring.

Keeshonden are excellent "doers" who thrive nicely on a sensible diet and are not "finicky" in their attitude towards food. A blessing in a busy household! They are hardy dogs, loving the snow and cold weather; but at the same time not overly sensitive to the discomforts of hot weather due to the splendid insulation against both extremes provided by their heavy coat.

Keeshonden can thrive well in city living, as their moderate size does not require excessive exercise. They are quite happy sharing your apartment, and are easily manageable dogs to walk on city streets, usually making friends and attracting attention by their good looks and obvious intelligence. They are admired wherever they go, both for their appearance and their manners.

This is a breed which is absolutely ideal for children of all ages. They are patient and loving with youngsters, at the same time being sufficiently strong and sturdy to not be easily hurt in play. Also their coat serves as a protection. They are not too big for even small children, and there is little if any danger of them accidentally knocking over or unintentionally hurting even a tiny toddler.

Their quiet temperament makes Keeshonden appeal to senior citizens for whom they make incomparable companions. Instinctively a gentle breed with great affection to bestow, they can brighten many a lonely person's life, as well as enhance that of a large and busy family.

Obviously Keeshonden are not attack dogs. This does not, however, mean that they are not capable watchdogs who will keep an alert ear and eye for sounds or signs of the alarming or unusual around your, and their, home.

A Keeshond's main purpose in life is to bring pleasure and companionship. He is a dog for people who love and enjoy having one around for the pleasure of its company, to share the daily life of household or an individual. He can bring endless cheer and freedom from loneliness. He can enhance your home and property, adding warmth, joy and beauty. He can teach your children the companionship of sharing life with a devoted canine friend, and help to raise them with an appreciation for his kind. He can make you proud and happy, if you are competitively inclined, in obedience and dog show competition. He loves to go in the car, on trips, for walks, wherever

(Left) Ch. Windrift's Lover Boy, by Ch. Rich-Bob's Stormy Weather, ROMX, ex Windrift's Lovelace, bred by Joanne Sanford Reed, owned by Les Baker. (Right) Ch. Gregory's Pittance of Tryon, ROM, by Gregory's Zilver Vox ex Am., Can. Ch. Tryon's Tuppence (litter sister to Ch. Tryon's Fearless Fruehling, ROMX, top producing Keeshond bitch in history). Bred by Donald R. Gregory. Owned by Dick and Joan F. Magliozzi, Big Rock, Illinois.

Ch. Windrift's Producer, by Ch. Star Kees Dingbat, C.D., HOF, ROMX ex Ch. Windrift's Academy Award, at his first show taking Best in Sweepstakes, Keeshond Club of Southern California Specialty and first in Bred-by Exhibitor (18 entries). Owned by Joanne Reed, Canyon Country, California. Bred by Joanne Reed and Jack and Arlene Grimes.

you may wish, so long as you are there. He lives to share with his master and his family.

Anyone who once has owned, or been closely acquainted with a Keeshond, becomes forevermore an enthusiast over the many charms and admirable qualities of these very superior dogs.

Purchasing Your Keeshond Puppy

It is never wise to just rush out and buy the first cute puppy who catches your eye. Whether you wish a dog to show, one with whom to compete in obedience, or one as a family dog purely for his (or her) companionship, the more time and thought you invest as you plan the purchase, the more likely you are to meet with complete satisfaction. The background and early care behind your pet will reflect in the dog's future health and temperament. Even if you are planning the purchase purely as a pet, with no thoughts of showing or breeding in the dog's or puppy's future, it is essential that if the dog is to enjoy a trouble-free future you assure yourself of a healthy, properly raised puppy or adult from sturdy, well-bred stock.

Throughout the pages of this book you will find the names and locations of many well-known and well-established kennels in various areas. Another source of information is the American Kennel Club (51 Madison Avenue, New York, New York 10010) from whom you can obtain a list of recognized breeders in the vicinity of your home. If you plan to have your dog campaigned by a professional handler, by all means let the handler help you locate and select a good dog. Through their numerous clients, handlers have access to a variety of interesting show prospects; and the usual arrangement is that the handler re-sells the dog to you for what his cost has been, with the agreement that the dog be campaigned for you by him throughout the dog's career. I most strongly recommend that prospective purchasers follow these suggestions, as you thus will be better able to locate and select a satisfactory puppy or dog.

Your first step in searching for your puppy is to make appointments at kennels specializing in the chosen breed, where you can visit and inspect the dogs, both those available for sale and the kennel's basic breeding stock. You are looking for an active, sturdy puppy with bright eyes and intelligent expression and who is friendly and alert; avoid puppies who are hyperactive, dull, or listless. The coat should be clean and thick, with no sign of parasites. The premises on which he was raised should look (and smell) clean and be tidy, making it obvious that the puppies and their surroundings are in capable hands. Should the kennels featuring the breed you intend owning be sparse in your area or not have what you consider attractive, do not hesitate to contact others at a distance and purchase from them if they seem better able to supply a puppy or dog who will please you *so long as it is a recognized breeding kennel of that breed.* Shipping dogs is a regular practice nowadays, with comparatively few problems when one considers the number of dogs shipped each year. A reputable, well-known breeder wants the customer to be satisfied; thus he will represent the puppy fairly. Should you not be pleased with the puppy upon arrival, a breeder such as I have described will almost certainly permit its return. A conscientious breeder takes real interest and concern in the welfare of the dogs he or she causes to be brought into the world. Such a breeder also is proud of a reputation for integrity. Thus on two counts, for the sake of the dog's future and the breeder's reputation, to such a person a *satisfied* customer takes precedence over a sale at any cost.

If your puppy is to be a pet or "family dog," I feel the earlier the age at which it joins your household the better. Puppies are weaned and ready to start out on their own, under the care of a sensible new owner, at about six weeks old; and if you take a young one, it is often easier to train it to the routine of your household and your requirements of it than is the case with an older dog which, even though still a puppy technically, may have already started habits you will find difficult to change. The younger puppy is usually less costly, too, as it stands to reason the breeder will not have as much expense invested in it. Obviously, a puppy that has been raised to five or six months old represents more in care and cash expenditure on the breeder's part than one sold earlier and therefore should be and generally is priced accordingly.

There is an enormous amount of truth in the statement that "bargain" puppies seldom turn out to be that. A "cheap" puppy, cheaply raised purely for sale and profit, can and often does lead to great heartbreak including problems and veterinarian's bills which can add up to many times the initial cost of a properly reared dog. On the other hand, just because a puppy is expensive does not assure one that is healthy and well reared. I know of numerous cases where unscrupulous dealers have sold for several hundred dollars puppies that were sickly, in poor condition, and such poor specimens that the

Ch. Windrift Fair N' Square, by Ch. Rich-Bob's Stormy Weather, ROMX, ex Windrift Lovelace, ROM, was bred by Joanne Reed and is co-owned by her with Mary Ellen Marxs. A Group 1 winner. Best of Breed at Westminster 1980. Winner of the Central States Keeshond Specialty in 1979.

Ronson's Playmate Pumkin, by Ch. Windrift's Lover Boy ex Ch. Conquest Penny Pitter Patter, has 14 points with two "majors" as we go to press. Bred by Ronald Fulton. Owned by Anna Seward, Jamestown, New York.

Keeshee Shantelle at eleven weeks. A fine representative of the Keeshee Keeshonden owned by C. and M. Sheehy, Riverwood, New South Wales, Australia.

breed of which they were supposedly members was barely recognizable. So one cannot always judge a puppy by price alone. Common sense must guide a prospective purchaser, plus the selection of a *reliable*, well-recommended dealer whom you know to have well satisfied customers or, best of all, a specialized breeder. You will probably find the fairest pricing at the kennel of a breeder. Such a person, experienced with the breed in general and with his or her own stock in particular, through extensive association with these dogs has watched enough of them mature to have obviously learned to assess quite accurately each puppy's potential—something impossible where such background is non-existent.

One more word on the subject of pets. Bitches make a fine choice for this purpose as they are usually quieter and more gentle than the males, easier to house train, more affectionate, and less inclined to roam. If you do select a bitch and have no intention of breeding or showing her, by all means have her spayed, for your sake and for hers. The advantages to the owner of a spayed bitch include avoiding the nuisance of "in season" periods which normally occur twice yearly, with the accompanying eager canine swains haunting your premises in an effort to get close to your female, plus the unavoidable messiness and spotting of furniture and rugs at this time, which can be annoying if she is a household companion in the habit of sharing your sofa or bed. As for the spayed bitch, she benefits as she grows older because this simple operation almost entirely eliminates the possibility of breast cancer ever occurring. I personally believe that all bitches should eventually be spayed—even those used for show or breeding when their careers are ended—in order that they may enjoy a happier, healthier old age. Please take note, however, that a bitch who has been spayed (or an altered dog) *cannot be shown at American Kennel Club Dog shows once this operation has been performed.* Be certain that you are *not* interested in showing her before taking this step.

Also in selecting a pet, never underestimate the advantages of an older dog, perhaps a retired show dog or a bitch no longer needed for breeding, who may be available quite reasonably priced by a breeder anxious to place such a dog in a loving home. These dogs are settled and can be a delight to own, as they make wonderful companions, especially in a household of adults where raising a puppy can sometimes be a trial.

Everything we have said about careful selection of your pet puppy and its place of purchase applies, but with many further considerations, when you plan to buy a show dog or foundation stock for a future breeding program. Now is the time for an in-depth study of the breed, starting with every word and every illustration in this book and all others you can find written on the subject. The standard of the breed now has become your guide, and you must learn not only the words but also how to interpret them and how they are applicable in actual dogs before you are ready to make an intelligent selection of a show dog.

If you are thinking in terms of a dog to show, obviously you must have learned about dog shows and must be in the habit of attending them. This is fine, but now your activity in this direction should be increased, with your attending every single dog show within a reasonable distance from your home. Much can be learned about a breed at ringside at these events. Talk with the breeders who are ex-

Ch. Windrift's Gambler, C.D., HOF, with the Best of Breed-Breeder Award he earned for Joanne Reed by winning the Keeshond Club of America National Specialty in 1982.

192

Ch. Shirtrai Puf'N Stuf of Nordeen, by Ch. Markitz Speculation ex Nordeen's Invincible Girl, was bred by Velva Bell Nordeen and is owned by Shirley Trainer, Oskaloosa, Iowa. Pictured in 1974 winning the Sweepstakes at Heart of America Keeshond Club Specialty judged by Eloise Geiger.

hibiting. Study the dogs they are showing. Watch the judging with concentration, noting each decision made and attempt to follow the reasoning by which the judge has reached it. Note carefully the attributes of the dogs who win and, for your later use, the manner in which each is presented. Close your ears to the ringside know-it-alls, usually novice owners of only a dog or two and very new to the Fancy, who have only derogatory remarks to make about all that is taking place unless they happen to win. This is the type of exhibitor who "comes and goes" through the Fancy and whose interest is usually of very short duration owing to lack of knowledge and dissatisfaction caused by the failure to recognize the need to learn. You, as a fancier who we hope will last and enjoy our sport over many future years, should develop independent thinking at this stage; you should learn to draw your own conclusions about the merits, or lack of them, seen before you in the ring and thus, sharpen your own judgment in preparation for choosing wisely and well.

Note carefully which breeders campaign winning dogs, not just an occasional isolated good one but consistent, homebred winners. It is from one of these people that you should select your own future "star."

If you are located in an area where dog shows take place only occasionally or where there are long travel distances involved, you will need to find another testing ground for your ability to select a worthy show dog. Possibly, there are some representative kennels raising this breed within a reasonable distance. If so, by all means ask permission of the owners to visit the kennels and do so when permission is granted. You may not necessarily buy then and there, as they may not have available what you are seeking that very day, but you will be able to see the type of dog being raised there and to discuss the dogs with the breeder. Every time you do this, you add to your knowledge. Should one of these kennels have dogs which especially appeal to you, perhaps you could reserve a show-prospect puppy from a coming litter. This is frequently done, and it is often worth waiting for a puppy, unless you have seen a dog with which you are truly greatly impressed and which is immediately available.

We have already discussed the purchase of a pet puppy. Obviously this same approach applies in a far greater degree when the purchase involved is a future show dog. The only place at which to purchase a show prospect is from a breeder who raises show-type stock; otherwise, you are almost certainly doomed to disappointment as the puppy

A male puppy, three and a half months old, at Windrift Kennels. Joanne Reed, Canyon Country, California.

matures. Show and breeding kennels obviously cannot keep all of their fine young stock. An active breeder-exhibitor is, therefore, happy to place promising youngsters in the hands of people also interested in showing and winning with them, doing so at a fair price according to the quality and prospects of the dog involved. Here again, if no kennel in your immediate area has what you are seeking, do not hesitate to contact top breeders in other areas and to buy at long distance. Ask for pictures, pedigrees, and a complete description. Heed the breeder's advice and recommendations, after truthfully telling exactly what your expectations are for the dog you purchase. Do you want something with which to win just a few ribbons now and then? Do you want a dog who can complete his championship? Are you thinking of the real "big time" (*i.e.,* seriously campaigning with Best of Breed, Group wins, and possibly even Best in Show as your eventual goal)? Consider it all carefully in advance; then honestly discuss your plans with the breeder. You will be better satisfied with the results if you do this, as the breeder is then in the best position to help you choose the dog who is most likely to come through for you. A breeder selling a show dog is just as anxious as the buyer for the dog to succeed, and the breeder will represent the dog to you with truth and honesty. Also, this type of breeder does not lose interest the moment the sale has been made but when necessary will be right there ready to assist you with beneficial advice and suggestions based on years of experience.

As you make inquiries of at least several kennels, keep in mind that show-prospect puppies are less expensive than mature show dogs, the latter often costing close to four figures, and sometimes more. The reason for this is that, with a puppy, there is always an element of chance, the possibility of its developing unexpected faults as it matures or failing to develop the excellence and quality that earlier had seemed probable. There definitely is a risk factor in buying a show-prospect puppy. Sometimes all goes well, but occasionally the swan becomes an ugly duckling. Reflect on this as you consider available puppies and young adults. It just might be a good idea to go with a more mature, though more costly, dog if one you like is available.

When you buy a mature show dog, "what you see is what you get"; and it is not likely to change beyond coat and condition which are dependent on your care. Also advantageous for a novice owner is the fact that a mature dog of show quality almost certainly will have received show ring training and probably match show experience, which will make your earliest handling ventures far easier.

Frequently it is possible to purchase a beautiful dog who has completed championship but who, owing to similarity in bloodlines, is not needed for the breeder's future program. Here you have the opportunity of owning a champion, usually in the two- to five-year-old range, which you can enjoy campaigning as a "special" (for Best of Breed competition) and which will be a settled, handsome dog for you and your family to enjoy with pride.

If you are planning foundation for a future kennel, concentrate on acquiring one or two really superior bitches. These need not necessarily be top show-quality, but they should represent your breed's finest producing bloodlines from a strain noted for producing quality, generation after generation. A proven matron who is already the dam

Two adorable and beautiful Kees babies from Australia. Keeshee Topper, (right); and Keeshee Shantelle are bred and owned by C. and M. Sheehy, Keeshee Keeshonden, Riverwood, New South Wales.

Ch. Flakkee Instant Replay in January 1983, age thirteen and a half years and still looking in Best in Show condition. Among the assets of the Keeshond as a breed to own is longevity! Flakkee Kennels, owners, Mr. and Mrs. Porter Washington, Lawndale, California.

An example of a Keeshond's pedigree chart.

PEDIGREE
OF

BREED: KEESHOND	SEX MALE
DATE OF BIRTH: 23RD FEBRUARY, 1977	
BRED BY: IDA AND ERNIE EVANS	

NAME: AUST. CH. MAKORO SIR BENJAMIN	Reg No 40163
COLOUR and MARKINGS: SILVER GREY	
OWNED BY: PETER AND LYNDA CHURCHWARD	

PARENTS	GRANDPARENTS	GREAT-GRANDPARENTS	GREAT-GREAT-GRANDPARENTS
SIRE: AUST. CH. COLIJN TOBY TYLER (N) No. 309632 Owned by: E. & I. EVANS	SIRE: CH. LEDWELL JASPER (IMP U.K.)	S. CH. WAAKZAAM WAAG (U.K.)	S. CH. SINTERKLAAS BRUSH NAME D. CH. WAAKZAAM WALTRAUTE
		D. LEDWELL FAVOUR (U.K.)	S. RUFFINO OF RHINEVALE D. LEDWELL CATASTROPHE
	DAM: COLIJN SHAKIRA (N)	S. CH. SPAARNEHOF ADONIS	S. CH. ENSIGN OF DUROYA (IMP UK) D. CH. DELKEES KANAU KATJA
		D. CH. KARUAH VENUS	S. CH. ENSIGN OF DUROYA (IMP UK) D. CH. KENDARI COVER GIRL
DAM: AUST. CH. AAK BABETTE (N) No. 321844 Owned by: E. & I. EVANS	SIRE: CH. LEDWELL JASPER (IMP U.K.)	S. CH. WAAKZAAM WAAG (U.K.)	S. CH. SINTERKLAAS BRUSH NAME D. CH. WAAKZAAM WALTRAUTE
		D. LEDWELL FAVOUR (U.K.)	S. RUFFINO OF RHINEVALE D. LEDWELL CATASTROPHE
	DAM: CH. COLIJN ELETHA (N)	S. CH. SPAARNEHOF ADONIS	S. CH. ENSIGN OF DUROYA (IMP UK) D. CH. DELKEES KANAU KATJA
		D. CH. COLIJN LEKKER DROOM	S. CH. KENDARI KIJDAG D. CH. KARUAH VENUS

I hereby certify that the above information is correct to the best of my knowledge and belief.

SIGNED: _____ DATE: _____

of show-type puppies is, of course, the ideal selection; but these are usually difficult to obtain, no one being anxious to part with so valuable an asset. You just might strike it lucky, though, in which case you are off to a flying start. If you cannot find such a matron available, select a young bitch of finest background from top producing lines who is herself of decent type, free of obvious faults, and of good quality.

Great attention should be paid to the pedigree of the bitch from whom you intend to breed. If not already known to you, try to see the sire and dam. It is generally agreed that someone starting with a breed should concentrate on a fine collection of top-flight bitches and raise a few litters from these before considering keeping one's own stud dog. The practice of buying a stud and then breeding everything you own or acquire to that dog does not always work out well. It is better to take advantage of the many noted sires who are available to be used at stud, who represent all of the leading strains, and in each case carefully to select the one who in type and pedigree seems most compatible to each of your bitches, at least for your first several litters.

To summarize, if you want a "family dog" as a companion, it is best to buy it young and raise it to the habits of your household. If you are buying a show dog, the more mature it is, the more certain you can be of its future beauty. If you are buying foundation stock for a kennel, then bitches are better, but they must be from the finest *producing* bloodlines.

When you buy a pure-bred dog that you are told is eligible for registration with the American Kennel Club, you are entitled to receive from the seller an application form which will enable you to register your dog. If the seller cannot give you the application form you should demand and receive an identification of your dog consisting of the name of the breed, the registered names and numbers of the sire and dam, the name of the breeder, and your dog's date of birth. If the litter of which your dog is a part is already recorded with the American Kennel Club, then the litter number is sufficient identification.

Do not be misled by promises of papers at some later date. Demand a registration application form or proper identification as described above. If neither is supplied, do not buy the dog. So warns the American Kennel Club, and this is especially important in the purchase of show or breeding stock.

Chapter 10

The Care of Your Keeshond Puppy

Your Puppy's Arrival

The moment you decide to be the new owner of a puppy is not one second too soon to start planning for the puppy's arrival in your home. Both the new family member and you will find the transition period easier if your home is geared in advance for the arrival.

The first things to be prepared are a bed for the puppy and a place where you can pen him up for rest periods. I am a firm believer that every dog should have a crate of its own from the very beginning, so that he will come to know and love it as his special place where he is safe and happy. It is an ideal arrangement, for when you want him to be free, the crate stays open. At other times you can securely latch it and know that the pup is safely out of mischief. If you travel with him, his crate comes along in the car; and, of course, in travelling by plane there is no alternative but to have a carrier for the dog. If you show your dog, you will want him upon occasion to be in a crate a good deal of the day. So from every consideration, a crate is a very sensible and sound investment in your puppy's future safety and happiness and for your own peace of mind.

The crates I recommend are the wooden ones with removable side panels, which are ideal for cold weather (with the panels in place to

Opposite page: Future Ch. Star-Kee's Dingbat at his first show when only seven months of age, taking Reserve Winners Dog at the Keeshond Club of Southern California Specialty. Joanne Reed, owner, Canyon Country, California.

keep out drafts) and in hot weather (with the panels removed to allow better air circulation). Wire crates are all right in the summer, but they give no protection from cold or drafts. I intensely dislike aluminum crates due to the manner in which aluminum reflects surrounding temperatures. If it is cold, so is the metal of the crate; if it is hot, the crate becomes burning hot. For this reason I consider aluminum crates neither comfortable nor safe.

When you choose the puppy's crate, be certain that it is roomy enough not to become outgrown. The crate should have sufficient height so the dog can stand up in it as a mature dog and sufficient area so that he can stretch out full length when relaxed. When the puppy is young, first give him shredded newspaper as a bed; the papers can be replaced with a mat or turkish towels when the dog is older. Carpet remnants are great for the bottom of the crate, as they are inexpensive and in case of accidents can be quite easily replaced. As the dog matures and is past the chewing age, a pillow or blanket in the crate is an appreciated comfort.

Sharing importance with the crate is a safe area in which the puppy can exercise and play. If you are an apartment dweller, a baby's playpen for a toy dog or a young puppy works out well; for a larger breed or older puppy use a portable exercise pen which you can then use later when travelling with your dog or for dog shows. If you have a yard, an area where he can be outside in safety should be fenced in prior to the dog's arrival at your home. This area does not need to be huge, but it does need to be made safe and secure. If you are in a suburban area where there are close neighbors, stockade fencing works out best as then the neighbors are less aware of the dog and the dog cannot see and bark at everything passing by. If you are out in the country where no problems with neighbors are likely to occur, then regular chain-link fencing is fine. For added precaution in both cases, use a row of concrete blocks or railroad ties inside against the entire bottom of the fence; this precludes or at least considerably lessens the chances of your dog digging his way out.

Be advised that if yours is a single dog, it is very unlikely that it will get sufficient exercise just sitting in the fenced area, which is what most of them do when they are there alone. Two or more dogs will play and move themselves around, but from my own experience, one by itself does little more than make a leisurely tour once around the area to check things over and then lies down. You must include a daily walk or two in your plans if your puppy is to be rugged and well. Exer-

Train your show prospect puppy to pose nicely at an early age, carefully stacked to show off to best advantage. This is Magic Myst Tin Lizzy V. Graywyn at eight and a half weeks, owned by Gloria Marcelli and Donna Gierach.

cise is extremely important to a puppy's muscular development and to keep a mature dog fit and trim. So make sure that those exercise periods, or walks, a game of ball, and other such activities, are part of your daily program as a dog owner.

If your fenced area has an outside gate, provide a padlock and key and a strong fastening for it, and use them, so that the gate can not be opened by others and the dog taken or turned free. The ultimate convenience in this regard is, of course, a door (unused for other purposes) from the house around which the fenced area can be enclosed, so that all you have to do is open the door and out into his area he goes. This arrangement is safest of all, as then you need not be using a gate, and it is easier in bad weather since then you can send the dog out without taking him and becoming soaked yourself at the same time. This is not always possible to manage, but if your house is arranged so that you could do it this way, I am sure you would never regret it due to the convenience and added safety thus provided. Fencing in the entire yard, with gates to be opened and closed whenever a caller, deliveryman, postman, or some other person comes on your property, really is not safe at all because people not used to gates and their importance are frequently careless about closing and latching *securely*. I know of many heartbreaking incidents brought about by some-one carelessly only half closing a gate which the owner had thought to be firmly latched and the dog wandering out. For greatest security a fenced *area* definitely takes precedence over a fenced *yard*.

The puppy will need a collar (one that fits now, not one to be grown into) and lead from the moment you bring him home. Both should be an appropriate weight and type for his size. Also needed are a feeding dish and a water dish, both made preferably of unbreakable material. Your pet supply shop should have an interesting assortment of these and other accessories from which you can choose. Then you will need grooming tools of the type the breeder recommends and some toys. One of the best toys is a beef bone, either rib, leg, or knuckle (the latter the type you can purchase to make soup), cut to an appropriate size for your puppy dog. These are absolutely safe and are great exercise for the teething period, helping to get the baby teeth quickly out of the way with no problems. Equally satisfactory is Nylabone® , a nylon bone that does not chip or splinter and that "frizzles" as the puppy chews, providing healthful gum massage. Rawhide chews are safe, too, *IF made in the United States*. There was a problem a few years back owing to the chemicals with which some foreign rawhide toys had been treated, since which time we have carefully avoided giving them to our own dogs. Also avoid plastics and any sort of rubber toys, *particularly* those with squeakers which the puppy may remove and swallow. If you want a ball for the puppy to use when playing with him, select one of very hard construction made for this purpose and do not leave it alone with him because he may chew off and swallow bits of the rubber. Take the ball with you when the game is over. This also applies to some of those "tug of war" type rubber toys which are fun when used with the two of you for that purpose but again should *not* be left behind for the dog to work on with his teeth. Bits of swallowed rubber, squeakers, and other such foreign articles can wreak great havoc in the intestinal tract—do all you can to guard against them.

Too many changes all at once can be difficult for a puppy. For at least the first few days he is with you, keep him on the food and feeding schedule to which he is accustomed. Find out ahead of time from the breeder what he feeds his puppies, how frequently, and at what times of the day. Also find out what, if any, food supplements the breeder has been using and recommends. Then be prepared by getting in a supply of the same food so that you will have it there when you

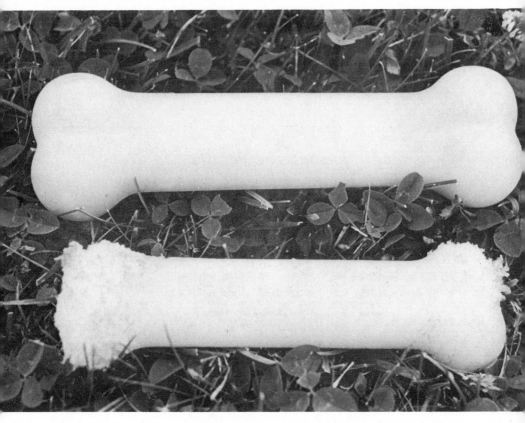

Nylabone is handled by most pet shops in the United States. It is a widely distributed pet product and exported to other countries, as well.

bring the puppy home. Once the puppy is accustomed to his new surroundings, then you can switch the type of food and schedule to fit your convenience, but for the first several days do it as the puppy expects.

Your selection of a veterinarian also should be attended to before the puppy comes home, because you should stop at the vet's office for the puppy to be checked over as soon as you leave the breeder's premises. If the breeder is from your area, ask him for recommendations. Ask your dog-owning friends for their opinions of the local veterinarians, and see what their experiences with those available have been. Choose someone whom several of your friends recommend highly, then contact him about your puppy, perhaps making an appointment to stop in at his office. If the premises are clean, modern, and well equipped, and if you like the veterinarian, make an appointment to bring the puppy in on the day of purchase. Be sure to obtain the puppy's health record from the breeder, including information on such things as shots and worming that the puppy has had.

Joining the Family

Remember that, exciting and happy an occasion as it is for you, the puppy's move from his place of birth to your home can be, for him, a traumatic experience. His mother and littermates will be missed. He quite likely will be awed or frightened by the change of surroundings. The person on whom he depended will be gone. Everything should be planned to make his arrival at your home pleasant—to give him confidence and to help him realize that yours is a pretty nice place to be after all.

Never bring a puppy home on a holiday. There just is too much going on with people and gifts and excitement. If he is in honor of an "occasion," work it out so that his arrival will be a few days earlier or, perhaps even better, a few days later than the "occasion." Then your home will be back to its normal routine and the puppy can enjoy your undivided attention. Try not to bring the puppy home in the evening. Early morning is the ideal time, as then he has the opportunity of getting acquainted and the initial strangeness should wear off before bedtime. You will find it a more peaceful night that way, I am sure. Allow the puppy to investigate as he likes, under your watchful eye. If you already have a pet in the household, keep a careful watch that the relationship between the two gets off to a friendly start or you may quickly find yourself with a lasting problem. Much of the future attitude of each toward the other will depend on what takes place that first day, so keep your mind on what they are doing and let your other activities slide for the moment. Be careful not to let your older pet become jealous by paying more attention to the puppy than to him, as that will start a bad situation immediately.

If you have a child, here again it is important that the relationship start out well. Before the puppy is brought home, you should have a talk with the youngster about puppies, so that it will be clearly understood that puppies are fragile and can easily be injured;

206

therefore, they should not be teased, hurt, mauled, or overly rough-housed. A puppy is not an inanimate toy; it is a living thing with a right to be loved and handled respectfully, treatment which will reflect in the dog's attitude toward your child as both mature together. Never permit your children's playmates to mishandle the puppy, as I have seen happen, tormenting the puppy until it turns on the children in self-defense. Children often do not realize how rough is too rough. You, as a responsible adult, are obligated to assure that your puppy's relationship with children is a pleasant one.

Do not start out by spoiling your puppy. A puppy is usually pretty smart and can be quite demanding. What you had considered to be "just for tonight" may be accepted by the puppy as "for keeps." Be firm with him, strike a routine, and stick to it. The puppy will learn more quickly this way, and everyone will be happier at the result. A radio playing softly or a dim night light are often comforting to a puppy as it gets accustomed to new surroundings and should be provided in preference to bringing the puppy to bed with you—unless, of course, you intend him to share the bed as a permanent arrangement

Socializing and Training Your New Puppy

Socialization and training of your puppy should start the very day of his arrival in your home. Never address him without calling him by name. A short, simple name is the easiest to teach as it catches the dog's attention quickly, so avoid elaborate call names. Always address the dog by the same name, not a whole series of pet names; the latter will only confuse the puppy.

Using his name clearly, call the puppy over to you when you see him awake and wandering about. When he comes, make a big fuss over him for being such a good dog. He thus will quickly associate the sound of his name with coming to you and a pleasant happening.

Several hours after the puppy's arrival is not too soon to start accustoming him to the feel of a light collar. He may hardly notice it; or he may struggle, roll over, and try to rub it off his neck with his paws. Divert his attention when this occurs by offering a tasty snack or a toy (starting a game with him) or by petting him. Before long he will have accepted the strange feeling around his neck and no longer appear aware of it. Next comes the lead. Attach it and then immediately take the puppy outside or otherwise try to divert his attention with things to see and sniff. He may struggle against the lead at first, biting at it and trying to free himself. Do not pull him with it at this point; just hold the end loosely and try to follow him if he starts off in any direction. Normally his attention will soon turn to investigating his surroundings if he is outside or you have taken him into an unfamiliar room in your house; curiosity will take over and he will become interested in sniffing around the surroundings. Just follow him with the lead slackly held until he seems to have completely forgotten about it; then try with gentle urging to get him to follow you. Don't be rough or jerk at him; just tug gently on the lead in short quick motions (steady pulling can become a battle of wills), repeating his name or trying to get him to follow your hand which is holding a bite of food or an interesting toy. If you have an older lead-trained dog, then it should be a cinch to get the puppy to follow along after *him*. In any event, the average puppy learns quite quickly and will soon be trotting along nicely on the lead. Once that point has been reached, the next step is to teach him to follow on your left side, or heel. Of course this will not likely be accomplished all in one day but should be done with short training periods over the course of several days until you are satisfied with the result.

During the course of house training your puppy, you will need to take him out frequently and at regular intervals: first thing in the morning directly from the crate, immediately after meals, after the puppy has been napping, or when you notice that the puppy is looking for a spot. Choose more or less the same place to take the puppy each time so that a pattern will be established. If he does not go immediately, do not return him to the house as he will probably relieve himself the moment he is inside. Stay out with him until he has finished; then be lavish with your praise for his good behavior. If you catch the puppy having an accident indoors, grab him firmly and rush him outside, sharply saying "No!" as you pick him up. If you do not see the accident occur, there is little point in doing anything except cleaning it up, as once it has happened and been forgotten, the puppy will most likely not even realize why you are scolding him.

With a small or moderate size breed, especially if you live in a big city or are away many hours at a time, having a dog that is trained to go on paper has some very definite advantages. To do this, one proceeds pretty much the same way as taking the puppy outdoors, except now you place the puppy on the newspaper at the proper time. The paper should always be kept in the same spot. An easy way to paper train a

Ch. vonRyan's Grand Slam as a puppy in a relaxed moment. Owned by Brian and Yvonne Gray, vonRyan Kennels, Saskatchewan, Canada.

An adorable Keeshond puppy, Ackline's Solo Gezang at eight weeks. Owned by Dr. and Mrs. Benjamin Ackerman, Hollywood, Florida.

puppy if you have a playpen for it or an exercise pen is to line the area with newspapers; then gradually, every day or so, remove a section of newspaper until you are down to just one or two. The puppy acquires the habit of using the paper; and as the prepared area grows smaller, in the majority of cases the dog will continue to use whatever paper is still available. My own experience, with dogs of small or moderate size is that this works out well. It is pleasant, if the dog is alone for an excessive length of time, to be able to feel that if he needs it the paper is there and will be used.

The puppy should form the habit of spending a certain amount of time in his crate, even when you are home. Sometimes the puppy will do this voluntarily, but if not it should be taught to do so, which is accomplished by leading the puppy over by his collar, gently pushing him inside, and saying firmly "Down" or "Stay." Whatever expression you use to give a command, stick to the very same one each time for each act. Repetition is the big thing in training—and so is association with what the dog is expected to do. When you mean "Sit" always say exactly that. "Stay" should mean *only* that the dog should remain where he receives the command. "Down" means something else again. Do not confuse the dog by shuffling the commands, as this will create training problems for you.

As soon as he has had his immunization shots, take your puppy with you whenever and wherever possible. There is nothing that will build a self-confident, stable dog like socialization, and it is extremely important that you plan and give the time and energy necessary for this whether your dog is to be a show dog or a pleasant, well-adjusted family member. Take your puppy in the car so that he will learn to enjoy riding and not become carsick as dogs may do if they are infrequent travelers. Take him anywhere you are going where you are certain he will be welcome: visiting friends and relatives (if they do not have housepets who may resent the visit), busy shopping centers (keeping him always on lead), or just walking around the streets of your town. If someone admires him (as always seems to happen when we are out with puppies), encourage the stranger to pet and talk with him. Socialization of this type brings out the best in your puppy and helps him to grow up with a friendly outlook, liking the world and its inhabitants. The worst thing that can be done to a puppy's personality is to overly shelter him. By keeping him always at home away from things and people unfamiliar to him you may be creating a personality problem for the mature dog that will be a cross for you to bear later on.

Feeding Your Keeshond

Time was when providing nourishing food for our dogs involved a far more complicated procedure than people now feel is necessary. The old school of thought was that the daily ration must consist of fresh beef, vegetables, cereal, egg yolks, and cottage cheese as basics with such additions as brewer's yeast and vitamin tablets on a daily basis.

During recent years, however, many minds have changed regarding this procedure. We still give eggs, cottage cheese, and supplements to the diet, but the basic method of feeding dogs has changed; and the change has been, in the opinion of many authorities, definitely for the better. The school of thought now is that you are doing your dogs a favor when you feed them some of the fine commercially prepared dog foods in preference to your own home-cooked concoctions.

The reason behind this new outlook is easily understandable. The dog food industry has grown to be a major one, participated in by some of the best known and most respected names in the American way of life. These trusted firms, it is agreed, turn out excellent products, so people are feeding their dog food preparations with confidence and the dogs are thriving, living longer, happier, and healthier lives than ever before. What more could we want?

There are at least half a dozen absolutely top-grade dry foods to be mixed with broth or water and served to your dog according to directions. There are all sorts of canned meats, and there are several kinds of "convenience foods," those in a packet which you open and dump out into the dog's dish. It is just that simple. The "convenience" foods are neat and easy to use when you are away from home, but generally speaking we prefer a dry food mixed with hot water or soup and meat. We also feel that the canned meat, with its added fortifiers, is more beneficial to the dogs than the fresh meat. However, the two can be alternated or, if you prefer and your dog does well on it, by all means use fresh ground beef. A dog enjoys changes in the meat part of his diet, which is easy with the canned food since all sorts of beef are available (chunk, ground, stewed, and so on), plus lamb, chicken, and even such concoctions as liver and egg, just plain liver flavor, and a blend of five meats.

There also is prepared food geared to every age bracket of your dog's life, from puppyhood on through old age, with special additions or modifications to make it particularly nourishing and beneficial. Our

Pup learning to eat, three to four weeks. One from the Ch. Windrift's Gambler, C.D. ex Ch. Windrift Academy Award litter owned by Jack and Arlene Grimes, Martinez, California.

grandparents, and even our parents, never had it so good where the canine dinner is concerned, because these commercially prepared foods are tasty and geared to meeting the dog's gastronomic approval.

Additionally, contents and nutrients are clearly listed on the labels, as are careful instructions for feeding just the right amount for the size, weight, and age of each dog.

With these foods we do not feel the addition of extra vitamins is necessary, but if you do there are several kinds of those, too, that serve as taste treats as well as being beneficial. Your pet supplier has a full array of them.

Of course there is no reason not to cook up something for your dog if you would feel happier doing so. But it seems to us unnecessary when such truly satisfactory rations are available with so much less trouble and expense.

How often you feed your dog is a matter of how it works out best for you. Many owners prefer to do it once a day. I personally think that two meals, each of smaller quantity, are better for the digestion and more satisfying to the dog, particularly if yours is a household member who stands around and watches preparations for the family meals. Do not overfeed. That is the shortest route to all sorts of problems. Follow directions and note carefully how your dog is looking. If your dog is overweight, cut back the quantity of food a bit. If the dog looks thin, then increase the amount. Each dog is an individual and the food intake should be adjusted to his requirements to keep him feeling and looking trim and in top condition.

From the time puppies are fully weaned until they are about twelve weeks old, they should be fed four times daily. From three months to six months of age, three meals should suffice. At six months of age the puppies can be fed two meals, and the twice daily feedings can be continued until the puppies are close to one year old, at which time feeding can be changed to once daily if desired.

If you do feed just once a day, do so by early afternoon at the latest and give the dog a snack, or biscuit or two, at bedtime.

Remember that plenty of fresh water should always be available to your puppy or dog for drinking. This is of utmost importance to his health.

"Almost, but not quite." Two young Kees owned by Brian and Yvonne Gray testing the possibilities of getting under the fence.

Anna Katherine Nicholas and Charlotte White with a handsome young Keeshond taking the points at Riverhead in 1977.

214

Chapter 11

The Making of a Show Dog

If you have decided to become a show dog exhibitor, you have accepted a very real and very exciting challenge. The groundwork has been accomplished with the selection of your future show prospect. If you have purchased a puppy, we assume that you have gone through all the proper preliminaries concerning good care, which should be the same if the puppy is a pet or future show dog with a few added precautions for the latter.

General Considerations

Remember the importance of keeping your future winner in trim, top condition. Since you want him neither too fat nor too thin, his appetite for his proper diet should be guarded, and children and guests should not be permitted to constantly be feeding him "goodies." The best treat of all is a small wad of raw ground beef or a packaged dog treat. To be avoided are ice cream, cake, cookies, potato chips, and other fattening items which will cause the dog to put on weight and may additionally spoil his appetite for the proper, nourishing, well-balanced diet so essential to good health and condition.

The importance of temperament and showmanship cannot possibly be overestimated. They have put many a mediocre dog across while lack of them can ruin the career of an otherwise outstanding specimen. From the day your dog joins your family, socialize him. Keep him accustomed to being with people and to being handled by people. Encourage your friends and relatives to "go over" him as the judges will in the ring so this will not seem a strange and upsetting experience.

Practice showing his "bite" (the manner in which his teeth meet) quickly and deftly. It is quite simple to slip the lips apart with your fingers, and the puppy should be willing to accept this from you or the judge without struggle. This is also true of further mouth examination when necessary. Where the standard demands examination of the roof of the mouth and the tongue, accustom the dog to having his jaws opened wide in order for the judge to make this required examination. When missing teeth must be noted, again, teach the dog to permit his jaws to be opened wide and his side lips separated as judges will need to check them one or both of these ways.

Some judges prefer that the exhibitors display the dog's bite and other mouth features themselves. These are the considerate ones, who do not wish to chance the spreading of possible infection from dog to dog with their hands on each one's mouth—a courtesy particularly appreciated in these days of virus epidemics. But the old fashioned judges still persist in doing it themselves, so the dog should be ready for either possibility.

Take your future show dog with you in the car, thus accustoming him to riding so that he will not become carsick on the day of a dog show. He should associate pleasure and attention with going in the car, or van or motor home. Take him where it is crowded: downtown, to the shops, everywhere you go that dogs are permitted. Make the expeditions fun for him by frequent petting and words of praise; do not just ignore him as you go about your errands.

Do not overly shelter your future show dog. Instinctively you may want to keep him at home where he is safe from germs or danger. This can be foolish on two counts. The first reason is that a puppy kept away from other dogs builds up no natural immunity against all the things with which he will come in contact at dog shows, so it is wiser actually to keep him well up to date on all protective shots and then let him become accustomed to being among dogs and dog owners. Also, a dog who never is among strange people, in strange places, or among strange dogs, may grow up with a shyness or timidity of spirit that will cause you real problems as his show career draws near.

Keep your show prospect's coat in immaculate condition with frequent grooming and daily brushing. When bathing is necessary, use a mild baby shampoo or whatever the breeder of your puppy may suggest. Several of the brand-name products do an excellent job. Be sure to rinse thoroughly so as not to risk skin irritation by traces of soap left behind and protect against soap entering the eyes by a drop of castor

The famed Keeshond Brace, owned by the Hempsteads and handled by D. Roy Holloway, being awarded Best Non-Sporting Brace at Westminster 1963.

oil in each before you lather up. Use warm water (be sure it is not uncomfortably hot or chillingly cold) and a good spray. A hair dryer is a real convenience for the heavily coated breeds and can be used for thorough drying after first blotting off the excess moisture with a turkish towel. A wad of cotton in each ear will prevent water entering the ear cavity.

Formation of mats should be watched for carefully if your breed is a heavily coated one, especially behind the ears and underneath the armpits. Toenails also should be watched and trimmed every few weeks. It is important not to permit nails to grow excessively long, as they will ruin the appearance of both the feet and pasterns.

Assuming that you will be handling the dog yourself, or even if he will be professionally handled, a few moments each day of dog show routine is important. Practice setting him up as you have seen the exhibitors do at the shows you've attended, and teach him to hold this position once you have him stacked to your satisfaction. If he is a small

This fine moving Keeshond, snapped at the 1980 Keeshond Club of Delaware Valley Specialty, is Ch. Rockhold Fanfare of Ramsgate owned by Elizabeth Ginsberg and Charlotte White, with Mrs. White handling.

breed that judges examine on a table, accustom him to this. Make the learning period pleasant by being firm but lavish in your praise when he responds correctly. Teach him to gait at your side at a moderate rate on a loose lead. When you have mastered the basic essentials at home, then hunt out and join a training class for future work. Training classes are sponsored by show-giving clubs in many areas, and their popularity is steadily increasing. If you have no other way of locating one, perhaps your veterinarian would know of one through some of his other clients; but if you are sufficiently aware of the dog show world to want a show dog, you will probably be personally acquainted with other people who will share information of this type with you.

Accustom your show dog to being in a crate (which you should be doing with a pet dog as well). He should relax in his crate at the shows "between times" for his own well being and safety.

A show dog's teeth must be kept clean and free of tartar. Hard dog-biscuits can help toward this, but if tartar accumulates, see that it is removed promptly by your veterinarian. Bones are not suitable for show dogs as they tend to damage and wear down the tooth enamel.

Grooming Your Keeshond for the Ring

by Carol Aubut

When one walks into a dog show ring for the first time, one is in awe of how beautiful the dogs looks. Most think this is how they look all the time, and have no idea how much homework must be done before the show.

Keeshonden are not a breed that has to be clipped, plucked or scissored. They do, however, require bathing—a full bath once a month, and a half bath before every show—and a fair amount of brushing. Brushing should be done thoroughly two or three times a week to maintain the coat. When giving a full bath, dry the excess water by blotting with a couple of large turkish bath towels; then place the dog on a grooming table and with a professional dog dryer "blow dry" the coat, brushing it until it is dry. Start at the top of the head, working your way back to the base of the tail. Then lay the dog on its side, start at the neck and work back to the hindquarters; repeat on the other side.

All coat on the body is brushed FORWARD. Let the dog stand up and he will shake himself, at which time the coat will fall into place. While the dog is standing, take each of its legs and brush the hair up. Take the tail in one hand and with the other hand using the brush, start at the base of the tail and brush all the hair towards the tip. Then go to the pants, brushing them with a downward motion.

When giving a half bath, wash the front legs, the back legs and pants, under the tail and the tail. This, too, should be brushed under the dryer until thoroughly dry.

There is very little trimming on a Keeshond; it is principally a matter of making the dog a bit neater. Trim the hair from between the pads of the feet, and around each foot, front and rear, so that no scraggly hairs appear to spoil the shape and tidy appearance. Trim the pasterns in a straight up and down motion in front, and do likewise to the hocks in the rear. Trimming whiskers is a matter of personal preference.

Any accumulated tartar on the teeth should be removed when necessary. You can do this yourself with a tooth scaler, working very carefully, or, if you prefer, have your veterinarian do the job for you, at least the first few times until you get the "hang" of it.

There is really no excuse for a judge ever being expected to examine a dirty or unkempt dog, and it is a pity when such a thing occurs, as a well-groomed Kees is such a beautiful dog.

The nails should be kept clipped short, both for the dog's comfort and for better movement. This, too, you can either do yourself or have it done by the veterinarian. It will be simpler if the dog is accustomed to having its nails clipped right from puppyhood.

You will need a grooming (rubber topped) table for your Kees, both to use at home and to take to the dog show. Other tools include a good pin brush; a slicker brush; scissors for trimming the feet; nail clippers; and a tooth scaler, and a good hair dryer.

In grooming your Kees, be sure always to brush the hair THOROUGHLY, from skin to tip, thus to avoid the formation of mats.

Match Shows

Your show dog's initial experience in the ring should be in match show competition for several reasons. First, this type of event is intended as a learning experience for both the dog and the exhibitor. You will not feel embarrassed or out of place no matter how poorly your puppy may behave or how inept your attempts at handling may be, as you will find others there with the same type of problems. The important thing is that you get the puppy out and into a show ring where the two of you can practice together and learn the ropes.

Only on rare occasions is it necessary to make match show entries in advance, and even those with a pre-entry policy will usually accept entries at the door as well. Thus you need not plan several weeks ahead, as in the case with point shows, but can go when the mood strikes you. Also there is a vast difference in the cost, as match show entries only cost a few dollars while entry fees for the point shows may be over ten dollars, an amount none of us needs to waste until we have some idea of how the puppy will behave or how much more pre-show training is needed.

Match shows very frequently are judged by professional handlers who, in addition to making the awards, are happy to help new exhibitors with comments and advice on their puppies and their presentation of them. Avail yourself of all these opportunities before heading out to the sophisticated world of the point shows.

Keeshonden seem to lend themselves especially well to Brace Class competition. These beauties, winning Non-Sporting Brace under William Kendrick, belong to Eloise Geiger and Marilyn Bender of North Canton, Ohio, and are handled here by Mrs. Geiger. August 1967.

Point Shows

As previously mentioned, entries for American Kennel Club point shows must be made in advance. This must be done on an official entry blank of the show-giving club. The entry must then be filed either personally or by mail with the show superintendent or the show secretary (if the event is being run by the club members alone and a superintendent has not been hired, this information will appear on the premium list) in time to reach its destination prior to the published closing date or filling of the quota. These entries must be made carefully, must be signed by the owner of the dog or the owner's agent (your professional handler), and must be accompanied by the entry fee; otherwise they will not be accepted. Remember that it is not when the entry leaves your hands that counts but the date of arrival at its destination. If you are relying on the mails, which are not always dependable, get the entry off well before the deadline to avoid disappointment.

A dog must be entered at a dog show in the name of the actual owner at the time of the entry closing date of that specific show. If a registered dog has been acquired by a new owner, it must be entered in the name of the new owner in any show for which entries close after the date of acquirement, regardless of whether the new owner has or has not actually received the registration certificate indicating that the dog is recorded in his name. State on the entry form whether or not transfer application has been mailed to the American Kennel Club, and it goes without saying that the latter should be attended to promptly when you purchase a registered dog.

In filling out your entry blank, type, print, or write clearly, paying particular attention to the spelling of names, correct registration numbers, and so on. Also, if there is more than one variety in your breed, be sure to indicate into which category your dog is being entered.

The Puppy Class is for dogs or bitches who are six months of age and under twelve months, were whelped in the United States, and are not champions. The age of a dog shall be calculated up to and inclusive of the first day of a show. For example, the first day a dog whelped on January 1st is eligible to compete in a Puppy Class at a show is July 1st of the same year; and he may continue to compete in Puppy Classes up to and including a show on December 31st of the same year, but he is *not* eligible to compete in a Puppy Class at a show held on or after January 1st of the following year.

222

Fairville's Round Trip taking a 3-point "major" at eleven months. Needs just another "major" to become a champion as of December 1983. Jean Toombs, owner, Wilmington, Delaware.

Ch. Dean's Shirtrai Jit Jot Roc pictured at the age of six and a half months, by Ch. Silva Thunder-On Van Rijn Aak ex Ch. Nordeen's Silver Keya Von Aak, C.D. Bred by Marc Avery and Claudia Wegener and owned by Shirley Trainer. Jit Jot Roc was # 10 Keeshond in the Nation for 1975.

Ch. Windrift's Lover Boy, by Ch. Rich-Bob's Stormy Weather, ROMX ex Windrift's Love Lace, ROM, has four Group firsts, nine additional Group placements, and three Specialty Bests of Breed at the close of 1983.

Ch. Japar Jubilation, one of the outstanding Kees winners owned by Dr. and Mrs. Benjamin Ackerman, handled by Joy S. Brewster, at Ox Ridge Kennel Club in September 1973.

The Puppy Class is the first one in which you should enter your puppy. In it a certain allowance will be made for the fact that they *are* puppies, thus an immature dog or one displaying less than perfect showmanship will be less severely penalized than, for instance, would be the case in Open. It is also quite likely that others in the class will be suffering from these problems, too. When you enter a puppy, be sure to check the classification with care, as some shows divide their Puppy Class into a 6-9 months old section and a 9-12 months old section.

The Novice Class is for dogs six months of age and over, whelped in the United States or Canada, who *prior to the official closing date for entries* have *not* won three first prizes in the Novice Class, any first prize at all in the Bred-by Exhibitor, American-bred, or Open Classes, or one or more points toward championship. The provisions for this class are confusing to many people, which is probably the reason exhibitors do not enter in it more frequently. A dog may win any number of first prizes in the Puppy Class and still retain his eligibility for Novice. He may place second, third or fourth not only in Novice on an unlimited number of occasions but also in Bred-by-Exhibitor, American-bred and Open and still remain eligible for Novice. But he may no longer be shown in Novice when he has won three blue ribbons in that class, when he has won even one blue ribbon in either Bred-by-Exhibitor, American-bred, or Open, or when he has won a single championship point.

In determining whether or not a dog is eligible for the Novice Class, keep in mind the fact that previous wins are calculated according to the official published date for closing of entries, not by the date on which you may actually have made the entry. So if in the interim, between the time you made the entry and the official closing date, your dog makes a win causing him to become ineligible for Novice, change your class *immediately* to another for which he will be eligible, preferably such as either Bred-by-Exhibitor or American-bred. To do this, you must contact the show's superintendent or secretary, at first by telephone to save time and at the same time confirm it in writing. The Novice Class always seems to have the fewest entries of any class, and therefore it is a splendid "practice ground" for you and your young dog while you are getting the "feel" of being in the ring.

Bred-by-Exhibitor Class is for dogs whelped in the United States or, if individually registered in the American Kennel Club Stud Book, for dogs whelped in Canada who are six months of age or older, are not champions, and are owned wholly or in part by the person or by the spouse of the person who was the breeder or one of the breeders of record. Dogs entered in this class must be handled in the class by an owner or by a member of the immediate family of the owner. Members of an immediate family for this purpose are husband, wife, father, mother, son, daughter, brother or sister. This is the class which is really the "breeders' showcase," and the one which breeders should enter with particular pride to show off their achievements.

The American-bred Class is for all dogs excepting champions, six months of age or older, who were whelped in the United States by reason of a mating which took place in the United States.

The Open Class is for any dog six months of age or older (this is the only restriction for this class). Dogs with championship points compete in it, dogs who are already champions are eligible to do so, dogs who are imported can be entered, and, of course, American-bred dogs compete in it. This class is, for some strange reason, the favorite of exhibitors who are "out to win." They rush to enter their pointed dogs in it, under the false impression that by doing so they assure themselves of greater attention from the judges. This really is not so, and in my opinion to enter in one of the less competitive classes, with a better chance of winning it and thus earning a second opportunity of gaining the judge's approval by returning to the ring in the Winners Class, can often be a more effective strategy.

One does not enter for the Winners Class. One earns the right to compete in it by winning first prize in Puppy, Novice, Bred-by-Exhibitor, American-bred, or Open. No dog who has been defeated on the same day in one of these classes is eligible to compete for Winners, and every dog who has been a blue-ribbon winner in one of them and not defeated in another, should he have been entered in more than one class, (as occasionally happens) *must* do so. Following the selection of the Winners Dog or the Winners Bitch, the dog or bitch receiving that award leaves the ring. Then the dog or bitch who placed second in that class, unless previously beaten by another dog or bitch in another class at the same show, re-enters the ring to compete against the remaining first-prize winners for Reserve. The latter award indicates that the dog or bitch selected for it is standing "in reserve" should the one who received Winners be disqualified or declared ineligible through any technicality when the awards are checked at the American Kennel Club. In that case, the one who placed Reserve is moved up to Winners, at the same time receiving the appropriate championship points.

Winners Dog and Winners Bitch are the awards which carry points toward championship with them. The points are based on the number of dogs or bitches actually in competition, and the points are scaled one through five, the latter being the greatest number available to any one dog or bitch at any one show. Three-, four-, or five-point wins are considered majors. In order to become a champion, a dog or bitch must have won two majors under two different judges, plus at least one point from a third judge, and the additional points necessary to bring the total to fifteen. When your dog has gained fifteen points as described above, a championship certificate will be issued to you, and your dog's name will be published in the champions of record list in the *Pure-Bred Dogs, American Kennel Gazette,* the official publication of the American Kennel Club.

The scale of championship points for each breed is worked out by the American Kennel Club and reviewed annually, at which time the number required in competition may be either changed (raised or lowered) or remain the same. The scale of championship points for all breeds is published annually in the May issue of the *Gazette,* and the current ratings for each breed within that area are published in every show catalog.

When a dog or bitch is adjudged Best of Winners, its championship points are, for that show, compiled on the basis of which sex had the greater number of points. If there are two points in dogs and four in bitches and the dog goes Best of Winners, then *both* the dog and the bitch are awarded an equal number of points, in this case four. Should the Winners Dog or the Winners Bitch go on to win Best of Breed or Best of Variety, additional points are accorded for the additional dogs and bitches defeated by so doing, provided, of course, that there were entries specifically for Best of Breed Competition or Specials, as these specific entries are generally called.

If your dog or bitch takes Best of Opposite Sex after going Winners, points are credited according to the number of the same sex defeated in both the regular classes and Specials competition. If Best of Winners is also won, then whatever additional points for each of these awards are available will be credited. Many a one- or two-point win has grown into a major in this manner.

Moving further along, should your dog win its Variety Group from the classes (in other words, if it has taken either Winners Dog or Winners Bitch), you then receive points based on the greatest number of points awarded to any member of any breed included within that Group during that show's competition. Should the day's winning also include Best in Show, the same rule of thumb applies, and your dog or bitch receives the highest number of points awarded to any other dog of any breed at that event.

Best of Breed competition consists of the Winners Dog and the Winners Bitch, who automatically compete on the strength of those awards, in addition to whatever dogs and bitches have been entered specifically for this class for which champions of record are eligible. Since July 1980, dogs who, according to their owner's records, have completed the requirements for a championship after the closing of entries for the show, but whose championships are unconfirmed, may be transferred from one of the regular classes to the Best of Breed competition, provided this transfer is made by the show superintendent or show secretary *prior to the start of any judging at the show.*

This has proved an extremely popular new rule, as under it a dog can finish on Saturday and then be transferred and compete as a Special on Sunday. It must be emphasized that the change *must* be made *prior* to the start of *any* part of the day's judging, not for just your individual breed.

In the United States, Best of Breed winners are entitled to compete in the Variety Group which includes them. This is not mandatory, it is a privilege which exhibitors value. (In Canada, Best of Breed winners *must* compete in the Variety Group, or they lose any points already won.) The dogs winning *first* in each of the seven Variety Groups *must* compete for Best in Show. Missing the opportunity of taking your dog in for competition in its Group is foolish as it is there where the general public is most likely to notice your breed and become interested in learning about it.

Non-regular classes are sometimes included at the all-breed shows, and they are almost invariably included at Specialty Shows. These include Stud Dog Class and Brood Bitch Class, which are judged on the basis of the quality of the two offspring accompanying the sire or dam. The quality of the latter two is beside the point and should not be considered by the judge; it is the youngsters who count, and the quality of *both* are to be averaged to decide which sire or dam is the best and most consistent producer. Then there is the Brace Class (which, at all-breed shows, moves up to Best Brace in each Variety Group and then Best Brace in Show), which is judged on the similarity and evenness of appearance of the two members of the brace. In other words, the two dogs should look like identical twins in size, color, and conformation

Ch. Flakkee Snapshot was the Top Winning Keeshond in the United States in 1982. Winner of eight Bests in Show, 39 Groups, 92 Bests of Breed. Another fine representative of Flakkee Kennels, Mr. and Mrs. Porter Washington, Lawndale, California.

Ch. Thrushwood's Foto Finish, C.D.X., six years of age, taking Best of Breed over other "specials." This was the first time he had been shown in breed competition since 1979. Handled by Sue Meyer for owner Barb Bagwell.

Ch. Vereeren of Vorden, magnificent Keeshond owned by Carl and Joseph Gettig, handled by D. Roy Holloway, taking Best in Show at Trenton Kennel Club in May 1968. John H. Cook, judge, Mrs. M. Lynwood Walton, Show Chairman, and Dr. Armour C. Wood, Club President.

Best Brood Bitch. Keeshond Club of Delaware Valley Specialty Show 1968, Jere R. Collins of England the judge. Ch. Rhapsody of Westcrest, ROM, with sons Ch. Fortune of Fairville, and Ch. Colonel Cinders of Fairville. Also came from Veterans Class to Best of Breed at the Capital Keeshond Club Specialty in 1969. Her last appearance was in the Veteran's Bitch Class at Keeshond Club of Delaware Valley Specialty in 1973 at twelve and a half years of age. She lived to an age of fifteen years and four months. Owned by Marguerite K. Goebel, Chadds Ford, Pa.

and should move together almost as a single dog, one person handling with precision and ease. The same applies to the Team Class competition, except that four dogs are involved and, if necessary, two handlers.

The Veterans Class is for the older dogs, the minimum age of whom is seven years. This class is judged on the quality of the dogs, as the winner competes in Best of Breed competition and has, on a respectable number of occasions, been known to take that top award. So the point is *not* to pick out the oldest dog, as some judges seem to believe, but the best specimen of the breed, exactly as in the regular classes.

Then there are Sweepstakes and Futurity Stakes sponsored by many Specialty clubs, sometimes as part of their regular Specialty Shows and sometimes as separate events on an entirely different occasion. The difference between the two stakes is that Sweepstakes entries usually include dogs from six to eighteen months age with entries made at the same time as the others for the show, while for a Futurity the entries are bitches nominated when bred and the individual puppies entered at or shortly following their birth.

If you already show your dog, if you plan on being an exhibitor in the future, or if you simply enjoy attending dog shows, there is a book, written by me, which you will find to be an invaluable source of detailed information about all aspects of show dog competition. This book is *Successful Dog Show Exhibiting* (T.F.H. Publications, Inc.) and is available wherever the one you are reading was purchased.

Junior Showmanship in Competition

If there is a youngster in your family between the ages of ten and sixteen, I can suggest no better or more rewarding hobby than becoming an active participant in Junior Showmanship. This is a marvelous activity for young people. It teaches responsibility, good sportsmanship, the fun of competition where one's own skills are the deciding factor of success, proper care of a pet, and how to socialize with other young folks. Any youngster may experience the thrill of emerging from the ring a winner and the satisfaction of a good job well done.

Entry in Junior Showmanship Classes is open to any boy or girl who is at least ten years old and under seventeen years old on the day of the show. The Novice Junior Showmanship Class is open to youngsters who have not already won, at the time the entries close, three firsts in this class. Youngsters who have won three firsts in Novice may compete in the Open Junior Showmanship Class. Any junior handler who wins his third first-place award in Novice may participate in the Open Class at the same show, provided that the Open Class has at least one other junior handler entered and competing in it that day. The Novice and Open Classes may be divided into Junior and Senior Classes. Youngsters between the ages of ten and twelve, inclusively, are eligible for the Junior division; and youngsters between thirteen and seventeen, inclusively, are eligible for the Senior division.

Any of the foregoing classes may be separated into individual classes for boys and for girls. If such a division is made, it must be so indicated on the premium list. The premium list also indicates the prize for Best Junior Handler, if such a prize is being offered at the show. Any youngster who wins a first in any of the regular classes may enter the competition for this prize, provided the youngster has been undefeated in any other Junior Showmanship Class at that show.

Junior Showmanship Classes, unlike regular conformation classes in which the quality of the dog is judged, are judged solely on the skill and ability of the junior handling the dog. Which dog is best is not the point—it is which youngster does the best job with the dog that is under consideration. Eligibility requirements for the dog being shown in Junior Showmanship, and other detailed information, can be found in *Regulations for Junior Showmanship*, available from the American Kennel Club.

A junior who has a dog that he or she can enter in both Junior Showmanship and conformation classes has twice the opportunity for success and twice the opportunity to get into the ring and work with the dog, a combination which can lead to not only awards for expert handling but also, if the dog is of sufficient quality, for making a conformation champion.

Pre-Show Preparations For Your Dog and You

Preparation of the items you will need as a dog show exhibitor should not be left until the last moment. They should be planned and arranged for at least several days in advance of the show in order for you to remain calm and relaxed as the countdown starts.

The importance of the crate has already been mentioned, and we hope it is already part of your equipment. Of equal importance is the grooming table, which very likely you have also already acquired for use at home. You should take it along with you to the shows, as your dog will need last minute touches before entering the ring. Should you have not yet made this purchase, folding tables with rubber tops are made specifically for this purpose and can be purchased at most dog shows, where concession booths with marvelous assortments of "doggy" necessities are to be found, or at your pet supplier. You will also need a sturdy tack box (also available at the dog show concessions) in which to carry your grooming tools and equipment. The latter should include brushes, comb, scissors, nail clippers, whatever you use for last minute clean-up jobs, cotton swabs, first-aid equipment, and anything you are in the habit of using on the dog, including a leash or two of the type you prefer, some well-cooked and dried-out liver or any of the small packaged "dog treats" for use as bait in the ring, an atomizer in case you wish to dampen your dog's coat when you are preparing him for the ring, and so on. A large turkish towel to spread under the dog on the grooming table is also useful.

Take a large thermos or cooler of ice, the biggest one you can accommodate in your vehicle, for use by "man and beast." Take a jug of water (there are lightweight, inexpensive ones available at all sporting goods shops) and a water dish. If you plan to feed the dog at the show, or if you and the dog will be away from home more than one day, bring food for him from home so that he will have the type to which he is accustomed.

You may or may not have an exercise pen. Personally I think one a *must*, even if you only have one dog. While the shows do provide areas for the exercise of the dogs, these are among the most likely places to have your dog come in contact with any illnesses which may be going around, and I feel that having a pen of your own for your dog's use is excellent protection. Such a pen can be used in other ways, too, such as a place other than the crate in which to put the dog to relax (that is roomier than the crate) and a place in which the dog can exercise at motels and rest areas. These, too, are available at the show concession stands and come in a variety of heights and sizes. A set of "pooper scoopers" should also be part of your equipment, along with a package of plastic bags for cleaning up after your dog.

Bring along folding chairs for the members of your party, unless all of you are fond of standing, as these are almost never provided anymore by the clubs. Have your name stamped on the chairs so that there will be no doubt as to whom the chairs belong. Bring whatever you and your family enjoy for drinks or snacks in a picnic basket or cooler, as show food, in general, is expensive and usually not great. You should always have a pair of boots, a raincoat, and a rain hat with

233

Am. and Can. Ch. Pied Piper of Fairville going Best of Breed over two major Canadian Specials at Barrie Kennel Club's prestigious show in Ontario, July 1981. Piper has multiple Group placements and many times has taken Best of Breed. Owned by Jean C. Toombs, Wilmington, Delaware.

you (they should remain permanently in your vehicle if you plan to attend shows regularly), as well as a sweater, a warm coat, and a change of shoes. A smock or big cover-up apron will assure that you remain tidy as you prepare the dog for the ring. Your overnight case should include a small sewing kit for emergency repairs, bandaids, headache and indigestion remedies, and any personal products or medications you normally use.

In your car you should always carry maps of the area where you are headed and an assortment of motel directories. Generally speaking, we have found Holiday Inns to be the nicest about taking dogs. Ramadas and Howard Johnsons generally do so cheerfully (with a few exceptions). Best Western generally frowns on pets (not always, but often

234

enough to make it necessary to find out which do). Some of the smaller chains welcome pets. The majority of privately owned motels do not.

Have everything prepared the night before the show to expedite your departure. Be sure that the dog's identification and your judging program and other show information are in your purse or briefcase. If you are taking sandwiches, have them ready. Anything that goes into the car the night before the show will be one thing less to remember in the morning. Decide upon what you will wear and have it out and ready. If there is any question in your mind about what to wear, try on the possibilities before the day of the show; don't risk feeling you may want to change when you see yourself dressed a few moments prior to departure time!

In planning your outfit, make it something simple that will not detract from your dog. Remember that a dark dog silhouettes attractively against a light background and vice-versa. Sport clothes always seem to look best at dog shows, preferably conservative in type and not overly "loud" as you do not want to detract from your dog, who should be the focus of interest at this point. What you wear on your feet is important. Many types of flooring can be hazardously slippery, as can wet grass. Make it a habit to wear rubber soles and low or flat heels in the ring for your own safety, especially if you are showing a dog that likes to move out smartly.

Your final step in pre-show preparation is to leave yourself plenty of time to reach the show that morning. Traffic can get amazingly heavy as one nears the immediate area of the show, finding a parking place can be difficult, and other delays may occur. You'll be in better humor to enjoy the day if your trip to the show is not fraught with panic over fear of not arriving in time!

Enjoying the Dog Show

From the moment of your arrival at the show until after your dog has been judged, keep foremost in your mind the fact that he is your reason for being there and that he should therefore be the center of your attention. Arrive early enough to have time for those last-minute touches that can make such a great difference when he enters the ring. Be sure that he has ample time to exercise and that he attends to personal matters. A dog arriving in the ring and immediately using it as an exercise pen hardly makes a favorable impression on the judge.

When you reach ringside, ask the steward for your arm-card and anchor it firmly into place on your arm. Make sure that you are where you should be when your class is called. The fact that you have picked up your arm-card does not guarantee, as some seem to think, that the judge will wait for you. The judge has a full schedule which he wishes to complete on time. Even though you may be nervous, assume an air of calm self-confidence. Remember that this is a hobby to be enjoyed, so approach it in that state of mind. The dog will do better, too, as he will be quick to reflect your attitude.

Always show your dog with an air of pride. If you make mistakes in presenting him, don't worry about it. Next time you will do better. Do not permit the presence of more experienced exhibitors to intimidate you. After all, they, too, once were newcomers.

The judging routine usually starts when the judge asks that the dogs be gaited in a circle around the ring. During this period the judge is watching each dog as it moves, noting style, topline, reach and drive, head and tail carriage, and general balance. Keep your mind and your eye on your dog, moving him at his most becoming gait and keeping your place in line without coming too close to the exhibitor ahead of you. Always keep your dog on the inside of the circle, between yourself and the judge, so that the judge's view of the dog is unobstructed.

Calmly pose the dog when requested to set up for examination whether on the ground or on a table. If you are at the head of the line and many dogs are in the class, go all the way to the end of the ring before starting to stack the dog, leaving sufficient space for those behind you to line theirs up as well as requested by the judge. If you are not at the head of the line but between other exhibitors, leave sufficient space ahead of your dog for the judge to examine him. The dogs should be spaced so that the judge is able to move among them to see them from all angles. In practicing to "set up" or "stack" your dog for the judge's examination, bear in mind the importance of doing so quickly and with dexterity. The judge has a schedule to meet and only a few moments in which to evaluate each dog. You will immeasurably help yours to make a favorable impression if you are able to "get it all together" in a minimum amount of time. Practice at home before a mirror can be a great help toward bringing this about, facing the dog so that you see him from the same side that the judge will and working to make him look right in the shortest length of time.

Listen carefully as the judge describes the manner in which the dog is to be gaited, whether it is straight down and straight back; down the ring, across, and back; or in a triangle. The latter has become the most popular pattern with the majority of judges. "In a triangle" means the dog should move down the outer side of the ring to the first corner, across that end of the ring to the second corner, and then back to the judge from the second corner, using the center of the ring in a diagonal line. Please learn to do this pattern without breaking at each corner to twirl the dog around you, a senseless maneuver we sometimes have noted. Judges like to see the dog in an uninterrupted triangle, as they are thus able to get a better idea of the dog's gait.

It is impossible to overemphasize that the gait at which you move your dog is tremendously important, and considerable study and thought should be given to the matter. At home, have someone move the dog for you at different speeds so that you can tell which shows him off to best advantage. The most becoming action almost invariably is seen at a moderate gait, head up and topline holding. Do not gallop your dog around the ring or hurry him into a speed atypical of his breed. Nothing being rushed appears at its best; give your dog a chance to move along at his (and the breed's) natural gait. For a dog's action to be judged accurately, that dog should move with strength and power but not excessive speed, holding a straight line as he goes to and from the judge.

As you bring the dog back to the judge, stop him a few feet away and be sure that he is standing in a becoming position. Bait him to show the judge an alert expression, using whatever tasty morsel he has been trained to expect for this purpose or, if that works better for you, use a small squeak-toy in your hand. A reminder, please, to those using liver or treats. Take them with you when you leave the ring. Do not just drop them on the ground where they will be found by another dog.

When the awards have been made, accept yours graciously, no matter how you actually may feel about it. What's done is done, and arguing with a judge or stomping out of the ring is useless and a reflection on your sportsmanship. Be courteous, congratulate the winner if your dog was defeated, and try not to show your disappointment. By the same token, please be a gracious winner; this, surprisingly, sometimes seems to be still more difficult.

Ronson's Thomas' Tamara To Love is the ONLY Keeshond to date to have achieved a T.D.X. title. This remarkable accomplishment was achieved with the training of owner Patricia Thomas, who "knew her Kees could do it" and proved her faith well justified! Tammie is by Ch. Windrift's Lover Boy ex Ch. Conquest Penny Pitter Patter.

238

Chapter 12

Your Keeshond and Obedience

For its own protection and safety, every dog should be taught, at the very least, to recognize and obey the commands "Come," "Heel," "Down," "Sit," and "Stay." Doing so at some time might save the dog's life and in less extreme circumstances will certainly make him a better behaved, more pleasant member of society. If you are patient and enjoy working with your dog, study some of the excellent books available on the subject of obedience and then teach your canine friend these basic manners. If you need the stimulus of working with a group, find out where obedience training classes are held (usually your veterinarian, your dog's breeder, or a dog-owning friend can tell you) and you and your dog can join up. Alternatively, you could let someone else do the training by sending the dog to class, but this is not very rewarding because you lose the opportunity of working with your dog and the pleasure of the rapport thus established.

If you are going to do it yourself, there are some basic rules which you should follow. You must remain calm and confident in attitude. Never lose your temper and frighten or punish your dog unjustly. Be quick and lavish with praise each time a command is correctly followed. Make it fun for the dog and he will be eager to please you by responding correctly. Repetition is the keynote, but it should not be continued without recess to the point of tedium. Limit the training sessions to ten- or fifteen-minute periods at a time.

Formal obedience training can be followed, and very frequently is, by entering the dog in obedience competition to work toward an obedience degree, or several of them, depending on the dog's aptitude and your own enjoyment. Obedience trials are held in conjunction with the majority of all-breed conformation dog shows, with Specialty shows, and frequently as separate Specialty events. If you are working alone with your dog, a list of trial dates might be obtained from your dog's veterinarian, your dog breeder, or a dog-owning friend; the A.K.C. *Gazette* lists shows and trials to be scheduled in the coming months; and if you are a member of a training class, you will find the information readily available.

The goals for which one works in the formal A.K.C. Member or Licensed Trials are the following titles: Companion Dog (C.D.), Companion Dog Excellent (C.D.X.), and Utility Dog (U.D.). These degrees are earned by receiving three "legs," or qualifying scores, at each level of competition. The degrees must be earned in order, with one completed prior to starting work on the next. For example, a dog must have earned C.D. prior to starting work on C.D.X.; then C.D.X. must be completed before U.D. work begins. The ultimate title attainable in obedience work is Obedience Trial Champion (O.T.Ch.).

When you see the letters "C.D." following a dog's name, you will know that this dog has satisfactorily completed the following exercises: heel on leash, heel free, stand for examination, recall, long sit and long stay. "C.D.X." means that tests have been passed on all of those just mentioned plus heel free, drop on recall, retrieve over high jump, broad jump, long sit, and long down. "U.D." indicates that the dog has additionally passed tests in scent discrimination (leather article), scent discrimination (metal article), signal exercises, directed retrieve, directed jumping, and group stand for examination. The letters "O.T.Ch." are the abbreviation for the only obedience title which precedes rather than follows a dog's name. To gain an obedience trial championship, a dog who already holds a Utility Dog degree must win a total of one hundred points and must win three firsts, under three different judges, in Utility and Open B Classes.

There is also a Tracking Dog title (T.D.) which can be earned at tracking trials. In order to pass the tracking tests the dog must follow the trail of a stranger along a path on which the trail was laid between thirty minutes and two hours previously. Along this track there must be more than two right-angle turns, at least two of which are well out in the open where no fences or other boundaries exist for the guidance of the dog or the handler. The dog wears a harness and is connected to the handler by a lead twenty to forty feet in length. Inconspicuously dropped at the end of the track is an article to be retrieved, usually a glove or wallet, which the dog is expected to locate and the handler to pick up. The letters "T.D.X." are the abbreviation for Tracking Dog Excellent, a more difficult version of the Tracking Dog test with a longer track and more turns to be worked through.

240

Owners of a Keeshonden have, over the years, been quick to appreciate the intelligence of their dogs and their trainability. Consequently right from the early 1930s, on until the present time, members of this breed have excelled in obedience rings as well as in conformation competition, and a very satisfactory number of them have been obedience "stars" as a result.

The first American C.D. Keeshond to our knowledge was an English dog who became Champion Herzog of Evenlode, C.D., following his importation from Miss Hastings' Evenlode Kennels by very enthusiastic early American fanciers, Mr. and Mrs. Richard Fort of Pleasantville, New York. A son of Champion Bingo ex Dorcas of Evenlode, Herzog was proudly advertised in the catalogue of the 1937 Westminster Kennel Club Dog Show as the "First Obedience Trained Keeshond in America"; thus he had completed his C.D. degree by that time.

From then on, there have been a steady succession of Kees proudly boasting combined titles and highest attainable obedience honors, as you will note as you read our kennel stories and the captions of the illustrations in this book. One of the most impressive and notable achievements in any breed of dog over the years was that, back in the early 1950s, of the magnificent Obedience Drill Team, consisting entirely of Keeshonden, which was organized and trained by the Milo Pearsalls who were themselves Kees owners. This team thrilled audiences wherever they were seen, defeated all others in competition at that time, and very deservedly earned for Mr. Pearsall the *Dog World Award for Distinguished Service* in 1953. It also provided some outstanding public education on the merits of the breed, as these fantastic dogs were popular guests on many a television show of those days. Betty and Ned Cummings, the popular professional handlers who were also Kees breeders of note, are among those whose dogs were part of this team.

Currently there are a number of extremely impressive records being attained in obedience by Keeshonden. Among the most successful fanciers in this field is Joy Ann Willding, owner of the Misazar Obedience Keeshonden at Schaumberg, Illinois. Joy owns three Kees who have gone High in Trial, among them the great Canadian Obedience Trial Champion Milmar's Center of Attention, U.D. "Gretchen," as this lovely bitch is called at home, was born on February 15th 1973,

Can. O.T.Ch. Milmar's Center of Attention and Jake's Mistake of Misazar, Am. and Can. C.D.X. Both owned, trained and handled by Joy-Ann Willding Misazar Obedience Keeshonden, Schaumberg, Illinois.

bred by Marilyn Miller, sired by Champion Milmar's Flying Dutchman ex Champion Car-Le-On's Precious Miss Priss. Her career started during 1975 in Novice, where she became Novice Dog of the Year, Rand Park Dog Training Club, with an average score of 196.

In 1976 she earned her C.D.X., averaging 197.5, and in 1977 she received her first Canadian High in Trial. 1978 found her Utility Dog of the Year, Rand Park Dog Training Club, with an average score of 192.17.

During 1979, Gretchen was shown 24 times in Open B, qualifying on thirteen occasions with an average score of 195.47. She received a Canadian High in Trial from Open B, and three times won first, had two seconds and three thirds. Thus she became # 2 Obedience Kees for that year, *Keezette* System; and # 6 Delaney System.

1980 found Gretchen in Open seventeen times, from which she qualified on six occasions, averaging 195.42. That same year she appeared seventeen times in Utility, qualifying eleven times with one second and four 4th placements, for an average of 193.64. That was the year in which she ranked # 4 in the *Keezette* System, was # 10 Non-Sporting Dog in Obedience in Canada, and received an American High in Trial.

In 1981, Gretchen was shown thirteen times in Open, qualifying nine times with an average of 195.86. Her Utility average was 194.14, shown in Utility 20 times, qualifying on six occasions.

Gretchen was inducted into the Keeshond Club of America Hall of Fame during that year, placed 5th in the Shuman System; 2nd in the *Keezette* System (her daughter beat her out for 1st); and 8th in the Delaney System.

Gretchen was officially retired in 1981 with 86 points towards an Obedience Trial Championship.

In 1982 she made a special appearance in Veteran's, scoring first with 198.

Jake's Mistake of Misazar, American and Canadian C.D.X., was bred by Dr. R. Stephen Willding and Joy Ann Willding and belongs to Joy Ann. She is Gretchen's daughter sired by Milmar's Matador of Karasar, and was born on July 1st 1976.

Jake's Mistake of Misazar, Am. and Can. C.D.X., by Milmar's Matador of Karasar ex Can. O.T. Ch. Milmar's Center of Attention, U.D., was born July 1st 1976. Bred by Dr. R. Stephen Willding and Joy-Ann Willding and owned by Joy Ann Willding.

Can. Ch. and O.T. Ch. Trial Ch. Tigger's Moonshadow, Can. and Am. U.D. at close to eight years of age, summer 1982. Owned by Tom and Ellen Crewe, Green Bay, Wisconsin.

Known as "Cricket," she won her Canadian Novice Degree in 1977. During the following year she was shown in Novice eleven times, qualifying 100 per cent of the time and averaging a score of 195.18. She received three times 1st prize, was second three times, and once took 3rd.

During 1979 Cricket competed three times in Graduate and qualified twice with two 1st places. Her Graduate Novice Average was 197.75.

1980 found Cricket shown seven times in Open A, qualifying five times. Her average was 195.90; her placements 2nd once and 3rd four times. During that year she earned a Canadian High in Trial.

Cricket was retired in 1981 at the close of a year in which she was shown 30 times, qualified fifteen times, and averaged 195.19. She placed 1st twice, 2nd, 3rd, and 4th once each.

Cricket placed # 2 in the Shuman System for 1981, and first in the *Keezette* System (where Gretchen, her Mom, was second).

And now we come to Mindy, who is Misazar's Attention Seeker, American C.D.X., Canadian C.D. She is Gretchen's granddaughter, being from Cricket and her sire is Champion Graywyn's Hot Shot. Born April 15th 1980, bred by Dr. R. Stephen Willding and Joy Ann Willding, owned by the latter.

Mindy's career started in 1982, when she was shown nine times, qualified 100 per cent of the time, placed 1st five times, placed 2nd and 4th on one occasion each, and twice was 3rd. She received one High in Trial that year, and gained # 2 place in the *Keezette* System. Her Novice average for 1982 was 197.67.

The following year in Open she averaged 196.33, and was shown in Open fifteen times qualifying on six of them, placing 1st and 2nd three times each. Also she was shown once in Novice that year placing second with 197.

During 1983, Mindy completed her Canadian C.D., received two High in Trial awards (one on the day she received her first leg in Open), and as of December, seems likely to wind up # 2 again in the *Keezette* System.

Another of the Obedience world's famous members is Canadian Champion and Obedience Trial Champion Tigger's Moonshadow, Canadian and American Utility Dog, owned, loved, and trained by Ellen Crewe of Green Bay, Wisconsin, who co-owns him with her husband, Tom. "Tigger" was bred by Clifton H. Toenges, was sired by Mayo Supreme from Sirocco's Glory, and was born on September 18th 1974. This dog is line-bred on Wistonia and Coventry.

In September 1979, when Tigger was five years old, Ellen Crewe first took him to Obedience school. She was told that he was "too old" for Ellen to ever hope to get a degree on him, but that if she wanted to come to classes she could do so. These people obviously were unacquainted with the Keeshond's desire to please or they would never have made that statement! Tigger won his American and Canadian Companion Dog degrees at his first three shows in both countries, averaging 192 in Canada and just under 188 in the United States.

In 1981 Ellen began showing Tigger in Open classes, Tigger gaining his Companion Dog Excellent in three straight shows, averaging just over 186. His Canadian C.D.X. took longer as he developed an aversion to the "drop on recall," but even so, he completed the degree in March of 1982 with a fourth place and an average just under 191.

Starting in the fall of 1982, Ellen and Tigger began the pursuit of Utility legs. Tigger's Canadian U.D./Obedience Trial Championship

"Tigger" in action. Showing excellent form, this is Can. Ch. and O.T. Ch. Tigger's Moonshadow, Can. and Am. U.D., proudly owned by Tom and Ellen Crewe, Green Bay, Wisconsin.

"Tigger" sitting at "front," the position the dog must go to when returning to his handler. Ellen Crewe, co-owner, trainer and handler, Green Bay, Wisconsin.

was completed with a 2nd, 3rd, and one 1st place, averaging 183.5, and finished when he was eight and a half years age in March 1983. His American U.D. was the hard one this time. Tigger loves to work, but NOT in high temperatures, and summer 1983 was no time to be showing in outdoor unshaded rings. However, as soon as the weather cooled off in September he put together the third leg, averaging 184.5, thus becoming only the THIRD Keeshond ever to hold both the American and the Canadian Utility Dog titles—and the second to do it with a conformation championship, too!

Barbara Bagwell at Hanna City, Illinois, owns Hi Struttin Banner Girl, C.D.X., a multiple High in Trial Dog. Also another top winning Obedience dog, Champion Thrushwood's Foto Finish, C.D.X.

Pat Thomas, Lansing, Michigan, owns the *only* T.D.X. Keeshond, Ronson's Thomas' Tamara To Love, C.D., T.D.X.

And there are a great many more constantly distinguishing themselves in a manner to bring pride to their breed and happiness to their owners.

Arlene Grimes has written us the story of her Mexican and International Champion ABC's Gypsy Silver, C.D.X., P.C.E. and Canadian C.D., which we feel will be of interest to our readers. (P.C.E. is Mexican C.D.) The following is told in Arlene's own words:

> Gypsy was whelped in Davis, California, a few days before I moved to San Jose to work with NASA. She was so named because of the frequency with which I would find her straying from her nest—before her eyes were open. She did most everything first in that litter, being the 'bright puppy' that all our visitors would pick out. I didn't intentionally keep her; we just sold all the others first. By that time I thought she had some promise as a show dog and she had us convinced that she would stay.
>
> Being Trophy Chairman for Nor-Cal Keeshond Club's Specialty, and a member of the host club, Contra Costa County Kennel Club, I was determined that obedience exhibitors would be treated to awards equal to the breed winners. I had arranged for silver-plated awards with a tea service for Highest Scoring Dog in Trial. Skoci (Gypsy's dam), my current contender, would be competing in Open, but her scores hadn't been quite so high as to realistically expect her to have a chance at it. From 1955 when I first

Mex. and Int. Ch. ABC's Gypsy Silver, C.D.X., P.C.E. (Mexican C.D.X.) and Can. C.D., by Ch. Wistonia Whiplee ex Silver Skoci of Rock Falls, C.D.X. and Can. C.D. Bred by Arlene Sloan (Grimes), owned by Jack and Arlene Grimes, Martinez, California.

started dog showing I had dreamed of having a dog win a silver tea set, any size, shape or design—I wasn't fussy.

Gypsy had been entered in Novice because it was the Specialty and she'd been in training for about the right length of time. Still a novice myself, I did not really think about whether she was "ready."

Came the day of the Specialty, Gypsy earned her first leg in obedience, in Novice with 199+ Can you imagine the tension, and ultimate elation, in winning a run-off and then discovering it was High in Trial??? I couldn't believe that the Paul Revere Tea Service was actually ours!

Two weeks later, with far fewer pressures, Gypsy IM-PROVED her score to 199½ for another High in Trial—and another tea set!

The following weekend Gypsy competed in the state of Washington (we were on our way to shows in British Columbia) to earn her third leg. All four of her Novice scores were first in class. She thus became the Keeshond Club of America's 1970 Top Winning Obedience Kees!

Then Gypsy's training began for Open work in 1973, which produced several non-qualifying scores.

1974 was to become a very good doggy year for the Grimes. In competing for Top Open Dog in Northern California, Gypsy had been mis-measured as 17½-¾. Consequently she jumped four boards instead of three for the broad jump, something she never before had been asked to do. She finished her Mexican and International conformation Championship titles in Mexico City as well as competing in two obedience classes at each show.

At various hours of the day we would work to improve performance—in darkness, rain, or on still summer nights. For practice we would play a game: I would tell her to "heel," then try to get away from her, using an unusual assortment of runs, turns, stops and slows. After a couple of minutes I'd quit. Gypsy would be sitting in perfect heel position smiling at me. She seemed to love the game. I'd laugh and she'd get excited, barking, and jumping. These extraordinary near-flawless performances that only I was witness to were easily the most thrilling with which Gypsy provided me.

These training "game" sessions paid off, for when Gypsy returned to the ring again competing in Open, she scored 198½ to a possible 200 points at the Keeshond Club of America Specialty in Open B, becoming Second Highest Scoring Dog in Trial; then a week later at Nor-Cal Specialty won 199 points in Open B and was Highest Scoring Dog in Trial; and the following day placed first with 197 points, again becoming Second Highest in Trial. During these three efforts she defeated a total of 300 other dogs.

Gypsy died of a brain tumor on September 1st 1977. During her career she won five *Dog World* Awards and her averages were, during her obedience career, 198.66 for C.D.; 198.33 for C.D.X. She was born March 2nd 1968, was bred by Arlene Sloan Grimes, and owned by Arlene and Jack Grimes. Gypsy was sired by Wistonia Whiplee ex

Silver Skoci of Rocky Falls, C.D.X. She was part of the first Keeshond litter bred by Arlene Grimes.

Gypsy's dam, Silver Skoci of Rocky Falls, C.D.X. and Canadian C.D., was acquired by Arlene Sloan prior to her marriage to Jack Grimes, back in 1966 when Skoci was four years old. Arlene had owned a Collie before that time, since 1955 to be exact, and had made some distinguished records with this bitch, whose name was Dawn.

In 1967 Skoci was High in Trial at the Sir Francis Drake Kennel Club with a score of 198 from judge James Frey from the Novice B Class, and the following month scored Second Highest in Trial with 198½. In 1968 Skoci was highly successful in obedience competition, and in 1969 earned her C.D.X. with scores of 197, 195, and 197 within two months' time. She also received a *Dog World* Award.

It is also worthy of note that when Gypsy took time off for motherhood she produced a son who did her and the Grimes proud.

Silver Skoci of Rocky Falls, C.D.X. winning Highest Scoring Dog in Trial, score 198, July 1970, Kelowna, British Columbia. Judge, M.J. Van DeKinder, right. Owned by Jack and Arlene Grimes, Martinez, California.

Ch. ABC's Zaffre Gypsy, C.D., by Ch. Zeedrift Kwikzilver ex Mex. and Int. Ch. ABC's Gypsy Silver, C.D.X., Mex. C.D.X. and Can. C.D. Breeders-owners, Jack and Arlene Grimes, Martinez, California.

This was Ch. ABC's **Zaffre Gypsy**, C.D., by Champion **Zeedrift Kwikzilver** from Gypsy, who started and finished his C.D. degree during 1974 and was Keeshond Club of America's Top Obedience Dog, owner-handled, for that year.

Arlene Grimes' pick of the litter which produced Zaffre was given by her to her husband, Jack, as her wedding present to him. Zev's fun match career began at four months of age, during which he "looked promising." He became an American Champion in 1973; a Mexican and International Champion in 1974; and a Canadian Champion in 1975. He was the Grimes' first Best of Breed winning dog, thus remains very special to them. Having promised her husband that "some day Zev would earn an obedience title," Arlene dared procrastinate no longer, so, at seven years of age, Zev started serious training. By late 1977 he had begun to get his act together, and in late 1978 he completed his C.D. degree, having had the shortest obedience career of any of the Grimes' dogs. His three trials averaged 194.66 at the age of eight and a half.

The local Parks and Recreation Commission (of Martinez) chose the year 1978 in which to discuss the ban of dogs from city parks. Zev quietly attended the three-and-a-half-hour meeting, making the point that use of city parks enabled him to come to that stage in his training. The Commission compromised by enacting a "pooper-scooper" ordinance.

Mrs. Grimes, who is a very experienced obedience teacher as well as trainer of her own dogs, makes the following observation:

> When most breeds of dogs are in obedience training, they
> are taught in a process of steps, *i.e.,* building the third step

251

upon the first and second. If as much as a week elapses without any training, most breeds have to be reviewed with at least the previously learned step, if not ALL the steps previously introduced. I found that with this particular Keeshond (Skoci, Gypsy's dam) and some subsequent others that:

1. If the handler can get the Kees to perform, however illogically, at step 3 or 4, there's not always a need to re-teach them steps 1 and 2, *i.e.*, that they can skip training steps, and:

2. Rather than seeing a performance deteriorate during/ after a break in training, I have seen a Kees behave as if there had not been a break in his/her training schedule, and even show advanced performance, *i.e.*, work as though the training schedule had been kept, and the dog advanced to the next logical step!

Kees generally do not forget what they've been taught; their retention is very much like the "elephant who never forgets."

In contrast to the extended training schedule of this first Kees of mine is the two-year-old male who received a "crash course" in Novice obedience because he was unruly around strange dogs. In four weeks' time he placed first in a Novice Y class of fifteen dogs. I was amazed!

Barbara Bagwell of Hanna City, Illinois, is the owner of two other very distinguished obedience Kees whose stories we share with you.

Hi Struttin Banner Girl, C.D.X., known as Fanci, was purchased by Barbara in 1974, a delight from the first day she was brought home. At the tender age of four months, she heeled on a show lead before formal showing training was ever begun. She was shown in obedience for the first time at the age of eight months, winning her first High in Match that day.

In 1975 Fanci received her C.D. and C.D.X. within a matter of six months, receiving a *Dog World* Award in both Novice and Open. She was High Keeshond in the Delaney System for the years 1975 through 1979, placing ninth in this sytem in the Non-Sporting Group in 1975, in 1976 was seventh and in 1977 was the fifth ranked dog in the Non-Sporting Group.

Am., Can., Mex., and Int. Ch. ABC's Gypsy Zev, C.D. in September 1974. Jack and Arelene Grimes, owners, Martinez, California.

In 1979, when *Keezette* magazine started its First Annual Awards System, Fanci was # 1, # 5 in 1980, not rated in 1980, and # 1 again in 1982.

In 1975 while attaining her Novice and Open degrees, Fanci had a ten-trial average of 197.85. In 1976 her average for thirteen trials was approximately the same, and she placed 1st, 2nd, or 3rd in all but two of the trials. In her career she scored 199½ twice, 199 five times, and had fourteen 198½s to her credit. She won High in Trial fifteen times. Fourteen were at all-breed obedience trials; the other High in Trial at the 1979 Keeshond Club of America National Specialty where she was presented with a beautiful pewter tea and coffee service for retiring the William G. Radell Memorial Trophy.

Fanci was shown in three Gaines Regional Tournaments and one Gaines Classic. She placed in each of the Gaines events in which she was shown.

Fanci was trained for Utility, but did not get her U.D. due to the development of a cataract. She was ten years old in January 1984 and enjoying retirement immensely as do most senior citizens.

Barbara Bagwell comments, " I have trained many dogs of various breeds, but Fanci will always be my special friend."

Barbara's other very distinguished winner is Champion Thrushwood's Foto Finish, C.D.X., who joined her family in 1977 at the age of eight weeks. He earned his conformation championship in 199 and was on hiatus until March 1981, when he was started in obedience training. Foto was shown only six times in Novice, and he placed six times, receiving a *Dog World* Award.

In August of 1981, Foto was shown at the Gaines Central Regional and placed tenth in the Novice Division. That year he was # 5 Keeshond for the Delaney System, # 5 Keeshond in the *Keezette* ratings, and # 1 Champion Obedience Dog for *Keezette* also.

1981 found him with a new trainer, Sherie Holm. Foto received his C.D.X. in five trials. He was # 4 dog according to the *Keezette* rating system, and again # 1 Champion Obedience Dog.

In 1983 Foto started showing in Open B. He was doing quite nicely with placements and a couple of outstanding scores when unfortunately his career was cut short by his untimely death at six years of age. How sad for such a tragic end to his life!

Barb Bagwell and Ch. Thrushwood's Foto Finish, C.D.X. placing #10, Novice Division, at the Gaines Central Regional, August 1981. His three scores over two days were 196½, 198 and 194½, for an average of 196 9/10.

Lachenhund Sunday Bonnet was Winners Bitch at Westminster 1978 at the Keeshond Club of Delaware Valley Specialty in 1975. Owned by Zoe W. Bemis of Bryn Mawr, Pennsylvania and Charlotte White of White Plains, Maryland.

Chapter 13

Breeding Your Keeshond

The Keeshond Brood Bitch

We have in an earlier chapter discussed selection of a bitch you plan to use for breeding. In making this important purchase, you will be choosing a bitch who you hope will become the foundation of your kennel. Thus she must be of the finest producing bloodlines, excellent in temperament, of good type, and free of major faults or unsoundness. If you are offered a "bargain" brood bitch, be wary, as for this purchase you should not settle for less than the best and the price will be in accordance with the quality.

Conscientious breeders feel quite strongly that the only possible reason for producing puppies is the ambition to improve and uphold quality and temperament within the breed—definitely *not* because one hopes to make a quick cash profit on a mediocre litter, which never seems to work out that way in the long run and which accomplishes little beyond perhaps adding to the nation's heartbreaking number of unwanted canines. The only reason ever for breeding a litter is, with conscientious people, a desire to improve the quality of dogs in their own kennel or, as pet owners, because they wish to add to the number of dogs they themselves own with a puppy or two from their present favorites. In either case breeding should not take place unless one has definitely prospective owners for as many puppies as the litter may contain, lest you find yourself with several fast-growing young dogs and no homes in which to place them.

Bitches should not be mated earlier than their second season, by which time they should be from fifteen to eighteen months old. Many breeders prefer to wait and first finish the championships of their show bitches before breeding them, as pregnancy can be a disaster to a show coat and getting the bitch back in shape again takes time. When you have decided what will be the proper time, start watching at least several months ahead for what you feel would be the perfect mate to best complement your bitch's quality and bloodlines. Subscribe to the magazines which feature your breed exclusively and to some which cover all breeds in order to familiarize yourself with outstanding stud dogs in areas other than your own for there is no necessity nowadays to limit your choice to a nearby dog unless you truly like him and feel that he is the most suitable. It is quite usual to ship a bitch to a stud dog a distance away, and this generally works out with no ill effects. The important thing is that you need a stud dog strong in those features where your bitch is weak or lacking and of bloodlines compatible to hers. Compare the background of both your bitch and the stud dog under consideration, paying particular attention to the quality of the puppies from bitches with backgrounds similar to your bitch's. If the puppies have been of the type and quality you admire, then this dog would seem a sensible choice for yours, too.

Stud fees may be a few hundred dollars, sometimes even more under special situations for a particularly successful sire. It is money well spent, however. Do *not* ever breed to a dog because he is less expensive than the others unless you honestly believe that he can sire the kind of puppies who will be a credit to your kennel and your breed.

Contacting the owners of the stud dogs you find interesting will bring you pedigrees and pictures which you can then study in relation to your bitch's pedigree and conformation. Discuss your plans with other breeders who are knowledgeable (including the one who bred your own bitch). You may not always receive an entirely unbiased opinion (particularly if the person giving it also has an available stud dog), but one learns by discussion so listen to what they say, consider their opinions, and then you may be better qualified to form your own opinion.

As soon as you have made a choice, phone the owner of the stud dog you wish to use to find out if this will be agreeable. You will be asked about the bitch's health, soundness, temperament, and freedom from serious faults. A copy of her pedigree may be requested, as might a picture of her. A discussion of her background over the telephone may be sufficient to assure the stud's owner that she is suitable for the stud dog and of type, breeding, and quality herself to produce puppies of the quality for which the dog is noted. The owner of a top-quality stud is often extremely selective in the bitches permitted to be bred to his dog, in an effort to keep the standard of his puppies high. The owner of a stud dog may require that the bitch be tested for brucellosis, which should be attended to not more than a month previous to the breeding.

Check out which airport will be most convenient for the person meeting and returning the bitch if she is to be shipped and also what airlines use that airport. You will find that the airlines are also apt to have special requirements concerning acceptance of animals for shipping. These include weather limitations and types of crates which are acceptable. The weather limits have to do with extreme heat and extreme cold at the point of destination, as some airlines will not fly dogs into temperatures above or below certain levels, fearing for their safety. The crate problem is a simple one, since if your own crate is not suitable, most of the airlines have specially designed crates available for purchase at a fair and moderate price. It is a good plan to purchase one of these if you intend to be shipping dogs with any sort of frequency. They are made of fiberglass and are the safest type to use for shipping.

Normally you must notify the airline several days in advance to make a reservation, as they are able to accommodate only a certain number of dogs on each flight. Plan on shipping the bitch on about her eighth or ninth day of season, but be careful to avoid shipping her on a weekend, when schedules often vary and freight offices are apt to be closed. Whenever you can, ship your bitch on a direct flight. Changing planes always carries a certain amount of risk of a dog being overlooked or wrongly routed at the middle stop, so avoid this danger if at all possible. The bitch must be accompanied by a health certificate which you must obtain from your veterinarian before taking her to the airport. Usually it will be necessary to have the bitch at the airport about two hours prior to flight time. Before finalizing arrangements, find out from the stud's owner at what time of day it will be most convenient to have the bitch picked up promptly upon arrival.

It is simpler if you can plan to bring the bitch to the stud dog. Some people feel that the trauma of the flight may cause the bitch to not conceive; and, of course, undeniably there is a slight risk in shipping which can be avoided if you are able to drive the bitch to her destination. Be sure to leave yourself sufficient time to assure your arrival at the right time for her for breeding (normally the tenth to fourteenth day following the first signs of color); and remember that if you want the bitch bred twice, you should allow a day to elapse between the two matings. Do not expect the stud's owner to house you while you are there. Locate a nearby motel that takes dogs and make that your head-quarters.

Just prior to the time your bitch is due in season, you should take her to visit your veterinarian. She should be checked for worms and should receive all the booster shots for which she is due plus one for parvo virus, unless she has had the latter shot fairly recently. The brucellosis test can also be done then, and the health certificate can be obtained for shipping if she is to travel by air. Should the bitch be at all overweight, now is the time to get the surplus off. She should be in good condition, neither underweight nor overweight, at the time of breeding.

The moment you notice the swelling of the vulva, for which you should be checking daily as the time for her season approaches, and the appearance of color, immediately contact the stud's owner and set-tle on the day for shipping or make the appointment for your arrival with the bitch for breeding. If you are shipping the bitch, the stud fee check should be mailed immediately, leaving ample time for it to have been received when the bitch arrives and the mating takes place. Be sure to call the airline making her reservation at that time, too.

Do not feed the bitch within a few hours before shipping her. Be certain that she has had a drink of water and been well exercised before closing her in the crate. Several layers of newspapers, topped with some shredded newspaper, make a good bed and can be discarded when she arrives at her destination; these can be replaced with fresh newspapers for her return home. Remember that the bitch should be brought to the airport about two hours before flight time as sometimes the airlines refuse to accept late arrivals.

If you are taking your bitch by car, be certain that you will arrive at a reasonable time of day. Do not appear late in the evening. If your ar-rival in town is not until late, get a good night's sleep at your motel and contact the stud's owner first thing in the morning. If possible, leave children and relatives at home, as they will only be in the way and perhaps unwelcome by the stud's owner. Most stud dog owners prefer not to have any unnecessary people on hand during the actual mating.

After the breeding has taken place, if you wish to sit and visit for awhile and the stud's owner has the time, return the bitch to her crate

260

Brood Bitch Class at a Keeshond Club of Southern California Specialty. Left to right, the dam, Ch. Traveler's Zeedrift Carioca with two of her kids. On the right, Ch. Flakkee's Snapshot, HOF, with owner Porter Washington. Center, Ch. Windrift's Midnite Masquerade. Breeders, Sandy Krueger and Joanne Reed.

in your car (first ascertaining, of course, that the temperature is comfortable for her and that there is proper ventilation. She should not be permitted to urinate for at least one hour following the breeding. This is the time when you get the business part of the transaction attended to. Pay the stud fee, upon which you should receive your breeding certificate and, if you do not already have it, a copy of the stud dog's pedigree. The owner of the stud dog does not sign or furnish a litter registration application until the puppies have been born.

Upon your return home, you can settle down and plan in happy anticipation a wonderful litter of puppies. A word of caution! Remember that although she has been bred, your bitch is still an interesting target for all male dogs, so guard her carefully for the next week or until you are absolutely certain that her season has entirely ended. This would be no time to have any unfortunate incident with another dog.

Ch. Keesland Firefly, male, by Ch. Gelderland Clipper of Swashway ex Ch. Ledwell Lustre of Keesland. Owned by Mrs. L. Goddard, bred by the Weedons, England.

Aust. Ch. Makoro Sir Benjamin, by Aust. Ch. Colijn Toby Tyler ex Aust. Ch. Aak Babette, born February 1977. Ida and Ernie Evans bred this noted dog who is owned by Peter and Lynda Churchward. Consistent winner at breed level in his younger days, Best in Show at the Non-Sporting and Working Group Club of South Australia, he is now a prominent winner of the Veterans Sweepstakes.

The Keeshond Stud Dog

Choosing the best stud dog to complement your bitch is often very difficult. The two principal factors to be considered should be the stud's conformation and his pedigree. Conformation is fairly obvious; you want a dog that is typical of the breed in the words of the standard of perfection. Understanding pedigrees is a bit more subtle since the pedigree lists the ancestry of the dog and involves individuals and bloodlines with which you may not be entirely familiar.

To a novice in the breed, then, the correct interpretation of a pedigree may at first be difficult to grasp. Study the pictures and text of this book and you will find many names of important bloodlines and members of the breed. Also make an effort to discuss the various dogs behind the proposed stud with some of the more experienced breeders, starting with the breeder of your own bitch. Frequently these folks will be personally familiar with many of the dogs in question, can offer opinions of them, and may have access to additional pictures which you would benefit by seeing.

It is very important that the stud's pedigree should be harmonious with that of the bitch you plan on breeding to him. Do not rush out and breed to the latest winner with no thought of whether or not he can produce true quality. By no means are all great show dogs great producers. It is the producing record of the dog in question and the dogs and bitches from which he has come which should be the basis on which you make your choice.

Breeding dogs is never a money-making operation. By the time you pay a stud fee, care for the bitch during pregnancy, whelp the litter, and rear the puppies through their early shots, worming, and so on, you will be fortunate to break even financially once the puppies have been sold. Your chances of doing this are greater if you are breeding for a show-quality litter which will bring you higher prices as the pups are sold as show prospects. Therefore, your wisest investment is to use the best dog available for your bitch regardless of the cost; then you should wind up with more valuable puppies. Remember that it is equally costly to raise mediocre puppies as top ones, and your chances of financial return are better on the latter. To breed to the most excellent, most suitable stud dog you can find is the only sensible thing to do, and it is poor economy to quibble over the amount you are paying in stud fee.

It will be your decision which course you decide to follow when you breed your bitch, as there are three options: line-breeding, inbreeding, and outcrossing. Each of these methods has its supporters and its detractors! Line-breeding is breeding a bitch to a dog belonging originally to the same canine family, being descended from the same ancestors, such as half-brother to half-sister, grandsire to grand-daughters, niece to uncle (and vice-versa) or cousin to cousin. Inbreeding is breeding father to daughter, mother to son, or full brother to sister. Outcross breeding is breeding a dog and a bitch with no or only a few mutual ancestors.

Line-breeding is probably the safest course, and the one most likely to bring results, for the novice breeder. The more sophisticated inbreeding should be left to the experienced, long-time breeders who thoroughly know and understand the risks and the possibilities involved with a particular line. It is usually done in an effort to intensify some ideal feature in that strain. Outcrossing is the reverse of inbreeding, an effort to introduce improvement in a specific feature needing correction, such as a shorter back, better movement, more correct head or coat, and so on.

It is the serious breeder's ambition to develop a strain or bloodline of their own, one strong in qualities for which their dogs will become distinguished. However, it must be realized that this will involve time, patience, and at least several generations before the achievement can be claimed. The safest way to enbark on this plan, as we have mentioned, is by the selection and breeding of one or two bitches, the best you can buy and from top-producing kennels. In the beginning you do *not* really have to own a stud dog. In the long run it is less expensive and sounder judgment to pay a stud fee when you are ready to breed a bitch than to purchase a stud dog and feed him all year; a stud dog does not win any popularity contests with owners of bitches to be bred until he becomes a champion, has been successfully Specialed for awhile, and has been at least moderately advertised, all of which adds up to a quite healthy expenditure.

The wisest course for the inexperienced breeder just starting out in dogs is as I have outlined above. Keep the best bitch puppy from the first several litters. After that you may wish to consider keeping your own stud dog if there has been a particularly handsome male in one of your litters that you feel has great potential or if you know where there is one available that you are interested in, with the feeling that he would work in nicely with the breeding program on which you have embarked. By this time, with several litters already born, your eye should have developed to a point enabling you to make a wise choice, either from one of your own litters or from among dogs you have seen that appear suitable.

The greatest care should be taken in the selection of your own stud dog. He must be of true type and highest quality as he may be responsible for siring many puppies each year, and he should come from a line of excellent dogs on both sides of his pedigree which themselves are, and which are descended from, successful producers. This dog should have no glaring faults in conformation; he should be of such quality that he can hold his own in keenest competition within his breed. He should be in good health, be virile and be a keen stud dog, a proven sire able to transmit his correct qualities to his puppies. Need I say that such a dog will be enormously expensive unless you have the good fortune to produce him in one of your own litters? To buy and use a lesser stud dog, however, is downgrading your breeding program unnecessarily since there are so many dogs fitting the description of a fine stud whose services can be used on payment of a stud fee.

You should *never* breed to an unsound dog or one with any serious standard or disqualifying faults. Not all champions by any means pass along their best features; and by the same token, occasionally you will find a great one who can pass along his best features but never gained his championship title due to some unusual circumstances. The information you need about a stud dog is what type of puppies he has produced and with what bloodlines and whether or not he possesses the bloodlines and attributes considered characteristic of the best in your breed.

If you go out to buy a stud dog, obviously he will not be a puppy but rather a fully mature and proven male with as many of the best attributes as possible. True, he will be an expensive investment, but if you choose and make his selection with care and forethought, he may well prove to be one of the best investments you have ever made.

Of course, the most exciting of all is when a young male you have decided to keep from one of your litters due to his tremendous show potential turns out to be a stud dog such as we have described. In this case he should be managed with care, for he is a valuable property that can contribute inestimably to his breed as a whole and to your own kennel specifically.

Do not permit your stud dog to be used until he is about a year old, and even then he should be bred to a mature, proven matron accustomed to breeding who will make his first experience pleasant and easy. A young dog can be put off forever by a maiden bitch who fights and resists his advances. Never allow this to happen. Always start a stud dog out with a bitch who is mature, has been bred previously, and is of even temperament. The first breeding should be performed in quiet surroundings with only you and one other person to hold the bitch. Do not make it a circus, as the experience will determine the dog's outlook about future stud work. If he does not enjoy the first experience or associates it with any unpleasantness, you may well have a problem in the future.

Your young stud must permit help with the breeding, as later there will be bitches who will not be cooperative. If right from the beginning you are there helping him and praising him whether or not your assistance is actually needed, he will expect and accept this as a matter of course when a difficult bitch comes along.

Things to have handy before introducing your dog and the bitch are K-Y jelly (the only lubricant which should be used) and a length of gauze with which to muzzle the bitch should it be necessary to keep her from biting you or the dog. Some bitches put up a fight; others are calm. It is best to be prepared.

At the time of the breeding the stud fee comes due, and it is expected that it will be paid promptly. Normally a return service is offered in case the bitch misses or fails to produce one live puppy. Conditions of the service are what the stud dog's owner makes them, and there are no standard rules covering this. The stud fee is paid for the act, not the result. If the bitch fails to conceive, it is customary for the owner to offer a free return service; but this is a courtesy and not to be considered a right, particularly in the case of a proven stud who is siring consistently and whose fault the failure obviously is *not*. Stud dog owners are always anxious to see their clients get good value and to have in the ring winning young stock by their dog; therefore, very few refuse to mate the second time. It is wise, however, for both parties to have the terms of the transaction clearly understood at the time of the breeding.

If the return service has been provided and the bitch has missed a second time, that is considered to be the end of the matter and the owner would be expected to pay a further fee if it is felt that the bitch should be given a third chance with the stud dog. The management of a stud dog and his visiting bitches is quite a task, and a stud fee has usually been well earned when one service has been achieved, let alone by repeated visits from the same bitch.

The accepted litter is one live puppy. It is wise to have printed a breeding certificate which the owner of the stud dog and the owner of the bitch both sign. This should list in detail the conditions of the breeding as well as the dates of the mating.

Upon occasion, arrangements other than a stud fee in cash are made for a breeding, such as the owner of the stud taking a pick-of-the-litter puppy in lieu of money. This should be clearly specified on the breeding certificate along with the terms of the age at which the stud's owner will select the puppy, whether it is to be a specific sex, or whether it is to be the pick of the entire litter.

The price of a stud fee varies according to circumstances. Usually, to prove a young stud dog, his owner will allow the first breeding to be quite inexpensive. Then, once a bitch has become pregnant by him, he becomes a "proven stud" and the fee rises accordingly for bitches that follow. The sire of championship-quality puppies will bring a stud fee of at least the purchase price of one show puppy as the accepted "rule-of-thumb." Until at least one champion by your stud dog has finished, the fee will remain equal to the price of one pet puppy. When his list of champions starts to grow, so does the amount of the stud fee. For a top-producing sire of champions, the stud fee will rise accordingly.

Almost invariably it is the bitch who comes to the stud dog for the breeding. Immediately upon having selected the stud dog you wish to use, discuss the possibility with the owner of that dog. It is the stud dog owner's prerogative to refuse to breed any bitch deemed unsuitable for his dog. Stud fee and method of payment should be stated at this time, and a decision reached on whether it is to be a full cash transaction at the time of the mating or a pick-of-the-litter puppy, usually at eight weeks of age.

If the owner of the stud dog must travel to an airport to meet the bitch and ship her for the flight home, an additional charge will be made for time, tolls, and gasoline based on the stud owner's proximity to the airport. The stud fee includes board for the day on the bitch's arrival through two days for breeding, with a day in between. If it is necessary that the bitch remain longer, it is very likely that additional board will be charged at the normal per-day rate for the breed.

Be sure to advise the stud's owner as soon as you know that your bitch is in season so that the stud dog will be available. This is especially important because if he is a dog being shown, he and his owner may be unavailable owing to the dog's absence from home.

As the owner of a stud dog being offered to the public, it is essential that you have proper facilities for the care of visiting bitches. Nothing can be worse than a bitch being insecurely housed and slipping out to become lost or bred by the wrong dog. If you are taking people's valued bitches into your kennel or home, it is imperative that you provide them with comfortable, secure housing and good care while they are your responsibility.

There is no dog more valuable than the proven sire of champions, Group winners and Best in Show dogs. Once you have such an animal, guard his reputation well and do *not* permit him to be bred to just any bitch that comes along. It takes two to make the puppies; even the most dominant stud can not do it all himself, so never permit him to breed a bitch you consider unworthy. Remember that when the puppies arrive, it will be your stud dog who will be blamed for any lack of quality, while the bitch's shortcomings will be quickly and conveniently overlooked.

Going into the actual management of the mating is a bit superfluous here. If you have had previous experience in breeding a dog and bitch you will know how the mating is done. If you do not have such experience, you should not attempt to follow directions given in a book but should have a veterinarian, breeder friend, or handler there to help you the first few times. You do not just turn the dog and bitch loose together and await developments, as too many things can go wrong and you may altogether miss getting the bitch bred. Someone should hold the dog and the bitch (one person each) until the "tie" is made and these two people should stay with them during the entire act.

If you get a complete tie, probably only the one mating is absolutely necessary. However, especially with a maiden bitch or one that has come a long distance for this breeding, we prefer following up with a second breeding, leaving one day in between the two matings. In this way there will be little or no chance of the bitch missing.

Once the tie has been completed and the dogs release, be certain that the male's penis goes completely back within its sheath. He should be allowed a drink of water and a short walk, and then he should be put into his crate or somewhere alone where he can settle down. Do not allow him to be with other dogs for a while as they will notice the odor of the bitch on him, and particularly with other males present, he may become involved in a fight.

Pregnancy, Whelping, and the Litter

Once the bitch has been bred and is back at home, remember to keep an ever watchful eye that no other male gets to her until at least the twenty-second day of her season has passed. Until then, it will still be possible for an unwanted breeding to take place, which at this point would be catastrophic. Remember that she actually can have two separate litters by two different dogs, so take care.

In other ways, she should be treated normally. Controlled exercise is good, and necessary for the bitch throughout her pregnancy, tapering it off to just several short walks daily, preferably on lead, as she reaches about her seventh week. As her time grows close, be careful about her jumping or playing too roughly.

The theory that a bitch should be overstuffed with food when pregnant is a poor one. A fat bitch is never an easy whelper, so the overfeeding you consider good for her may well turn out to be the exact opposite. During the first few weeks of pregnancy, your bitch should be fed her normal diet. At four to five weeks along, calcium should be added to her food. At seven weeks her food may be increased if she seems to crave more than she is getting, and a meal of canned milk (mixed with an equal amount of water) should be introduced. If she is fed just once a day, add another meal rather than overload her with too much at one time. If twice a day is her schedule, then a bit more food can be added to each feeding.

Ch. Windrift's Academy Award in February 1983, two days before whelping. Jack and Arlene Grimes, owners, Martinez California.

A week before the pups are due, your bitch should be introduced to her whelping box so that she will be accustomed to it and feel at home there when the puppies arrive. She should be encouraged to sleep there but permitted to come and go as she wishes. The box should be roomy enough for her to lie down and stretch out but not too large lest the pups have more room than is needed in which to roam and possibly get chilled by going too far away from their mother. Be sure that the box has a "pig rail"; this will prevent the puppies from being crushed against the sides. The room in which the box is placed, either in your home or in the kennel, should be kept at about 70 degrees Fahrenheit. In winter it may be necessary to have an infrared lamp over the whelping box, in which case be careful not to place it too low or close to the puppies.

Newspapers will become a very important commodity, so start collecting them well in advance to have a big pile handy to the whelping box. With a litter of puppies, one never seems to have papers enough, so the higher pile to start with, the better off you will be. Other necessities for whelping time are clean, soft turkish towels, scissors, and a bottle of alcohol.

You will know that her time is very near when your bitch becomes restless, wandering in and out of her box and of the room. She may refuse food, and at that point her temperature will start to drop. She will dig at and tear up the newspapers in her box, shiver, and generally look uncomfortable. Only you should be with your bitch at this time. She does not need spectators; and several people, even though they may be family members whom she knows, hanging over her may upset her to the point where she may harm the puppies. You should remain nearby, quietly watching, not fussing or hovering; speak calmly and frequently to her to instill confidence. Eventually she will settle down

Lunch time! The lovely Ch. Windrift's Academy Award relaxes while the babies (by Ch. Windrift's Gambler) enjoy a snack. Jack and Arlene Grimes, owners, Martinez, California.

in her box and begin panting; contractions will follow. Soon thereafter a puppy will start to emerge, sliding out with the contractions. The mother immediately should open the sac, sever the cord with her teeth, and then clean up the puppy. She will also eat the placenta, which you should permit. Once the puppy is cleaned, it should be placed next to the bitch unless she is showing signs of having the next one immediately. Almost at once the puppy will start looking for a nipple on which to nurse, and you should ascertain that it is able to latch on successfully.

If the puppy is a breech (*i.e.,* born feet first), you must watch carefully for it to be completely delivered as quickly as possible and the sac removed quickly so that the puppy does not drown. Sometimes even a normally positioned birth will seem extremely slow in coming. Should this occur, you might take a clean towel and, as the bitch contracts, pull the puppy out, doing so gently and with utmost care. If, once the puppy is delivered, it shows little signs of life, take a rough turkish towel and massage the puppy's chest by rubbing quite briskly back and forth. Continue this for about fifteen minutes, and be sure that the mouth is free from liquid. It may be necessary to try mouth-to-mouth breathing, which is done by pressing the puppy's jaws open and, using a finger, depressing the tongue which may be stuck to the roof of the mouth. Then place your mouth against the puppy's and blow hard down the puppy's throat. Bubbles may pop out of its nose, but keep on blowing. Rub the puppy's chest with the towel again and try artificial respiration, pressing the sides of the chest together slowly and rhythmically—in and out, in and out. Keep trying one method or the other for at least twenty minutes before giving up. You may be rewarded with a live puppy who otherwise would not have made it.

If you are successful in bringing the puppy around, do not immediately put it back with the mother as it should be kept extra warm. Put it in a cardboard box on an electric heating pad or, if it is the time of year when your heat is running, near a radiator or near the fireplace or stove. As soon as the rest of the litter has been born it then can join the others.

An hour or more may elapse between puppies, which is fine so long as the bitch seems comfortable and is neither straining nor contracting. She should not be permitted to remain unassisted for more than an hour if she does continue to contract. This is when you should get her to your veterinarian, whom you should already have alerted to the possibility of a problem existing. He should examine her and perhaps give her a shot of Pituitrin. In some cases the veterinarian may find that a Caesarean section is necessary due to a puppy being lodged in a manner making normal delivery impossible. Sometimes this is caused by an abnormally large puppy, or it may just be that the puppy is simply turned in the wrong position. If the bitch does require a Caesarean section, the puppies already born must be kept warm in their cardboard box with a heating pad under the box.

Once the section is done, get the bitch and the puppies home. Do not attempt to put the puppies in with the bitch until she has regained consciousness as she may unknowingly hurt them. But do get them back to her as soon as possible for them to start nursing.

Should the mother lack milk at this time, the puppies must be fed by hand, kept very warm, and held onto the mother's teats several times a day in order to stimulate and encourage the secretion of milk, which should start shortly.

Assuming that there has been no problem and that the bitch has whelped naturally, you should insist that she go out to exercise, staying just long enough to make herself comfortable. She can be offered a bowl of milk and a biscuit, but then she should settle down with her family. Freshen the whelping box for her with fresh newspapers while she is taking this respite so that she and the puppies will have a clean bed.

Unless some problem arises, there is little you must do about the puppies until they become three to four weeks old. Keep the box clean and supplied with fresh newspapers the first few days, but then turkish towels should be tacked down to the bottom of the box so that the puppies will have traction as they move about.

If the bitch has difficulties with her milk supply, or if you should be so unfortunate as to lose her, then you must be prepared to either hand-feed or tube-feed the puppies if they are to survive. We personally prefer tube-feeding as it is so much faster and easier. If the bitch is available, it is best that she continues to clean and care for the puppies in the normal manner excepting for the food supplements you will provide. If it is impossible for her to do this, then after every feeding you must gently rub each puppy's abdomen with wet cotton to make it urinate, and the rectum should be gently rubbed to open the bowels.

Newborn puppies must be fed every three to four hours around the clock. The puppies must be kept warm during this time. Have your veterinarian teach you how to tube-feed. You will find that it is really quite simple.

This promising (and endearing) Kees puppy is Wistonia Wyndham, by Ch. Windrift's Willy Weaver ex Ch. Wistonia Wyndixie, a future "star" recently purchased by Mrs. Zoe W. Bemis.

After a normal whelping, the bitch will require additional food to enable her to produce sufficient milk. In addition to being fed twice daily, she should be given some canned milk several times each day.

When the puppies are two weeks old, their nails should be clipped, as they are needle sharp at this age and can hurt or damage the mother's teats and stomach as the pups hold on to nurse.

Between three and four weeks of age, the puppies should begin to be weaned. Scraped beef (prepared by scraping it off slices of beef with a spoon so that none of the gristle is included) may be offered in very small quantities a couple of times daily for the first few days. Then by the third day you can mix puppy chow with warm water as directed on the package, offering it four times daily. By now the mother should be kept away from the puppies and out of the box for several hours at a time so that when they have reached five weeks of age she is left in with them only overnight. By the time the puppies are six weeks old, they should be entirely weaned and receiving only occasional visits from their mother.

Most veterinarians recommend a temporary DHL (distemper, hepatitis, leptospirosis) shot when the puppies are six weeks of age. This remains effective for about two weeks. Then at eight weeks of

Magic Myst Tin Lizzie V. Graywyn at eight and a half weeks old. Sired by Ch. Komaga's Sitting Bull ex Klassic's Kreation of Graywyn. Breeder, Joann Gray. Owner, Gloria Marcelli and Donna Gierach.

age, the puppies should receive the series of permanent shots for DHL protection. It is also a good idea to discuss with your vet the advisability of having your puppies inoculated against the dreaded parvovirus at the same time. Each time the pups go to the vet for shots, you should bring stool samples so that they can be examined for worms. Worms go through various stages of development and may be present in a stool sample even though the sample does not test positive in every checkup. So do not neglect to keep careful watch on this.

The puppies should be fed four times daily until they are three months old. Then you can cut back to three feedings daily. By the time the puppies are six months of age, two meals daily are sufficient. Some people feed their dogs twice daily throughout their lifetime; others go to one meal daily when the puppy becomes one year of age.

The ideal age for puppies to go to their new homes is between eight and twelve weeks, although some puppies successfully adjust to a new home when they are six weeks old. Be sure that they go to their new owners accompanied by a description of the diet you've been feeding them and a schedule of the shots they have already received and those they still need. These should be included with the registration application and a copy of the pedigree.

Ch. Chalice's Silver Horizon, handsome homebred dog owned by Cynthia Nary, Gig Harbor, Washington, here is winning Best in Show at the Kennel Club of Buffalo, July 1983, handled by Douglas R. Holloway.

Chapter 14

Travelling with Your Dog

When you travel with your dog, to shows or on vacation or wherever, remember that everyone does not share our enthusiasm or love for dogs and that those who do not, strange creatures though they seem to us, have their rights, too. These rights, on which we should not encroach, include not being disturbed, annoyed, or made uncomfortable by the presence and behavior of other people's pets. Your dog should be kept on lead in public places and should recognize and promptly obey the commands "Down," "Come," "Sit," and "Stay."

Take along his crate if you are going any distance with your dog. And keep him in it when riding in the car. A crated dog has a far better chance of escaping injury than one riding loose in the car should an accident occur or an emergency arise. If you do permit your dog to ride loose, never allow him to hang out a window, ears blowing in the breeze. An injury to his eyes could occur in this manner. He could also become overly excited by something he sees and jump out, or he could lose his balance and fall out.

Never, ever under any circumstances, should a dog be permitted to ride loose in the back of a pick-up truck. I have noted, with horror, that some people do transport dogs in this manner, and I think it cruel and shocking. How easily such a dog can be thrown out of the truck by sudden jolts or an impact! And I am sure that many dogs have jumped out at the sight of something exciting along the way. Some unthinking individuals tie the dog, probably not realizing that were he to jump under those circumstances, his neck would be broken, he could be dragged alongside the vehicle, or he could be hit by another vehicle. If you are for any reason taking your dog in an open back truck, please have sufficient regard for that dog to at least provide a crate for him, and then remember that, in or out of a crate, a dog riding under the direct rays of the sun in hot weather can suffer and have his life endangered by the heat.

If you are staying at a hotel or motel with your dog, exercise him somewhere other than in the flower beds and parking lot of the property. People walking to and from their cars really are not thrilled at "stepping in something" left by your dog. Should an accident occur, pick it up with a tissue or a paper towel and deposit it in a proper receptacle; do not just walk off leaving it to remain there. Usually there are grassy areas on the sides of and behind motels where dogs can be exercised. Use them rather than the more conspicuous, usually carefully tended, front areas or those close to the rooms. If you are becoming a dog show enthusiast, you will eventually need an exercise pen to take with you to the show. Exercise pens are ideal to use when staying at motels, too, as they permit you to limit the dog's roaming space and to pick up after him more easily.

Ch. Fearless Fieldmarshall, by Ch. Travelers Fearless Forecast ex Ch. Fearless Flowerchild, bred by Hellen Curtis and owned by Joan F. and A.R. Magliozzi.

Never leave your dog unattended in the room of a motel unless you are absolutely, positively certain that he will stay there quietly and not damage or destroy anything. You do not want a long list of complaints from irate guests, caused by the annoying barking or whining of a lonesome dog in strange surroundings or an overzealous watch dog barking furiously each time a footstep passes the door or he hears a sound from an adjoining room. And you certainly do not want to return to torn curtains or bedspreads, soiled rugs, or other embarrassing evidence of the fact that your dog is not really house-reliable after all.

If yours is a dog accustomed to travelling with you and you are positive that his behavior will be acceptable when left alone, that is fine. But if the slightest uncertainty exists, the wise course is to leave him in the car while you go to dinner or elsewhere; then bring him into the room when you are ready to retire for the night.

When you travel with a dog, it is often simpler to take along from home the food and water he will need rather than buying food and looking for water while you travel. In this way he will have the rations to which he is accustomed and which you know agree with him, and there will be no fear of problems due to different drinking water. Feeding on the road is quite easy now, at least for short trips, with all the splendid dry prepared foods and high-quality canned meats available. A variety of lightweight, refillable water containers can be bought at many types of stores.

If you are going to another country, you will need a health certificate from your veterinarian for each dog you are taking with you, certifying that each has had rabies shots within the required time preceding your visit.

Be careful always to leave sufficient openings to ventilate your car when the dog will be alone in it. Remember that during the summer, the rays of the sun can make an inferno of a closed car within only a few minutes, so leave enough window space open to provide air circulation. Again, if your dog is in a crate, this can be done quite safely. The fact that you have left the car in a shady spot is not always a guarantee that you will find conditions the same when you return. Don't forget that the position of the sun changes in a matter of minutes, and the car you left nicely shaded half an hour ago can be getting full sunlight far more quickly than you may realize. So, if you leave a dog in the car, make sure there is sufficient ventilation and check back frequently to ascertain that all is well.

Am., Mex., Can. and Int. Ch. ABC's Gypsy Zev, C.D. at eleven years of age, May 1981. Jack and Arelene Grimes, owners, Martinez, California.

Chapter 15

Responsibilities of Breeders and Owners

The first responsibility of any person breeding dogs is to do so with care, forethought, and deliberation. It is inexcusable to breed more litters than you need to carry on your show program or to perpetuate your bloodlines. A responsible breeder should not cause a litter to be born without definite plans for the safe and happy disposition of the puppies.

A responsible dog breeder makes absolutely certain, so far as is humanly possible, that the home to which one of his puppies will go is a good home, one that offers proper care and an enthusiastic owner. I have tremendous admiration for those people who insist on visiting (although doing so is not always feasible) the prospective owners of their puppies, to see if they have suitable facilities for keeping a dog, that they understand the responsibility involved, and that all members of the household are in accord regarding the desirability of owning one. All breeders should carefully check out the credentials of prospective purchasers to be sure that the puppy is being placed in responsible hands.

I am certain that no breeder ever wants a puppy or grown dog he has raised to wind up in an animal shelter, in an experimental laboratory, or as a victim of a speeding car. While complete control of such a situation may be impossible, it is at least our responsibility to make every effort to turn over dogs to responsible people. When selling a puppy, it is a good idea to do so with the understanding that should it become necessary to place the dog in other hands, the purchaser will first contact you, the breeder. You may want to help in some way, possibly by buying or taking back the dog or placing it elsewhere. It is not fair just

Two great and beautiful Kees bitches, Ch. Von Storm's Emaris *(left)* and Ch. Wallbridge's Best Bet, owned (and dearly loved) by Nancy P. Riley, Millport, New York.

to sell our puppies and then never again give a thought to their welfare. Family problems arise, people may be forced to move where dogs are prohibited, or people just plain grow bored with a dog and its care. Thus the dog becomes a victim. You, as the dog's breeder, should concern yourself with the welfare of each of your dogs and see to it that the dog remains in good hands.

The final obligation every dog owner shares, be there just one dog or an entire kennel involved, is that of making detailed, explicit plans for the future of our dearly loved animals in the event of the owner's death. Far too many of us are apt to procrastinate and leave this very important matter unattended to, feeling that everything will work out or that "someone will see to them." The latter is not too likely, at least not to the benefit of the dogs, unless you have done some advance planning which will assure their future well-being.

Life is filled with the unexpected, and even the youngest, healthiest, most robust of us may be the victim of a fatal accident or sudden illness. The fate of our dogs, so entirely in our hands, should never be left to chance. If you have not already done so, please get together with your lawyer and set up a clause in your will specifying what you want done with each of your dogs, to whom they will be entrusted (after first making absolutely certain that the person selected is willing and able to assume the responsibility), and telling the locations of all registration papers, pedigrees, and kennel records. Just think of the possibilities which might happen otherwise! If there is another family member who shares your love of the dogs, that is good and you have less to worry about. But if your heirs are not dog-oriented, they will hardly know how to proceed or how to cope with the dogs themselves, and they may wind up disposing of or caring for your dogs in a manner that would break your heart were you around to know about it.

In our family, we have specific instructions in each of our wills for each of our dogs. A friend, also a dog person who regards her own dogs with the same concern and esteem as we do ours, has agreed to take over their care until they can be placed accordingly and will make certain that all will work out as we have planned. We have this person's name and phone number prominently displayed in our van and car and in our wallets. Our lawyer is aware of this fact. It is all spelled out in our wills. The friend has a signed check of ours to be used in case of an emergency or accident when we are travelling with the dogs; this check will be used to cover her expense to come and take over the care of our dogs should anything happen to make it impossible for us to do so. This, we feel, is the least any dog owner should do in preparation for the time our dogs suddenly find themselves without us. There have been so many sad cases of dogs unprovided for by their loving owners, left to heirs who couldn't care less and who disposed of them in any way at all to get rid of them, or left to heirs who kept and neglected them under the misguided idea that they were providing them "a fine home with lots of freedom." All of us *must* prevent any of these misfortunes befalling our own dogs who have meant so much to us!

Index